Lynette Carr Armstrong

Lynette Carr Armstrong has been an English, Drama and Media teacher and adviser for nearly thirty years. She has taught in a variety of London schools and worked in a number of local authorities focusing on school improvement, leadership, wider curriculum development and assessment.

Samantha Wharton

Samantha Wharton has been a teacher for over eighteen years and currently teaches English at St Angela's Ursuline, an outstanding secondary school in East London. She has a degree in Communications and Media (Brunel University), a PGCE in English and Drama (from the Institute of Education, University London) and an MA in Black British Literature (from Goldsmiths University). As an educator, Samantha has strived to empower and encourage her students to broaden their imaginations through a love of literature. She is committed to ensuring that her students are given options that are diverse and reflective of the world we live in.

**Study Guides
from Nick Hern Books**

GCSE Study Guides
Winsome Pinnock's *Leave Taking*
Chinonyerem Odimba's *Princess & The Hustler*

Page to Stage Study Guides
Jessica Swale's *Blue Stockings*
Henrik Ibsen's *A Doll's House*
Diane Samuels' *Kindertransport*
Timberlake Wertenbaker's *Our Country's Good*
Anton Chekhov's *Three Sisters*

GCSE STUDY GUIDE

FOR ENGLISH LITERATURE

Winsome Pinnock's

LEAVE TAKING

*Lynette Carr Armstrong
and Samantha Wharton*

NICK HERN BOOKS

London
www.nickhernbooks.co.uk

A Nick Hern Book

Leave Taking: The GCSE Study Guide
first published in Great Britain in 2024 by Nick Hern Books Ltd,
The Glasshouse, 49a Goldhawk Road, London W12 8QP

Cover image: Sarah Niles as Enid and Seraphina Beh as Del in the 2018 revival
of *Leave Taking* at the Bush Theatre, London. Photo by Helen
Murray/ArenaPAL (www.arenapal.com)

Designed and typeset by Nick Hern Books, London

Printed and bound in Great Britain by
Mimeo Ltd, Huntingdon, Cambs PE29 6XX

A CIP catalogue record for this book is available from the British Library

ISBN 978 1 83904 136 5

Contents

Foreword
Winsome Pinnock

My mother migrated from Jamaica to the United Kingdom in 1959, following her husband-to-be who, like Enid's spouse in *Leave Taking*, saved his salary for a whole year before he was able to afford the money to buy a ticket for her passage over. The shock and disappointment of those who migrated to the UK at that time is well documented. My parents' generation had been indoctrinated by a colonialist education that lionised all things British. They celebrated Empire Day (24th May) when their schools distributed British flags and lollipops. Despite their disappointment on entering a country whose environment was often hostile ('No blacks, no dogs, no Irish!'), they didn't complain and rarely discussed the hardships. After all, they had grown up on plantation villages where the legacy of enslavement was still evident in the wretched poverty they endured. Jamaica achieved independence the year that my youngest sibling was born. My parents' marriage disintegrated a few years later, and my mother became a single parent to four young children at a time when there was still stigma attached to divorce.

Writers are given their preoccupations at birth. I am the descendant of enslaved Africans who were forcibly denied the right to the written word, or to express themselves through art or song and yet held on to aspects of their African heritage in both. Traces of African spiritual rituals were preserved by clandestine practices like obeah, which was made illegal in Jamaica in 1898, a law that remains on the statute books. Despite its illegality, my mother and some of her peers retained an interest in obeah, consulting obeah men and women in times of crisis for advice and healing.

At university I was told that, although I was considered a talented actress, I probably wouldn't be cast in many productions because I was black. I focused on my writing. I had started writing a play (a sketch really) about two girls getting ready to go out but never managing to leave their bedroom. I sent it to the Royal Court Young Writers' Group and was invited to join. It was there that I wrote *Leave Taking*, my first full-length play, when I was twenty-three years old. I wanted to make Enid the heroine of the play because I couldn't recall ever seeing such a character – a hospital cleaner – as the lead in a British play. I specifically wanted to write about the black British experience as distinct from African American culture because producers often seemed to think that they are interchangeable.

At the Royal Court Young Writers' Group we were encouraged by workshop leaders Hanif Kureishi and Stephen Wakelam to 'write what you know'. I now understand that you write what you come to know. Writing is an exploration, the pursuit of the answer to an unanswerable question. I started out wanting to write about the daughters – this new breed of black British woman – but ended up fascinated by Enid and the complexity of her relationship with England, her daughters, and herself, as well as her long-standing friendship with Brod whom she has known since childhood.

After the first performances of the play at the Liverpool Playhouse Studio women from different cultural backgrounds collared me to say: 'That's my story. I'm Enid,' or 'That's my mam. She's just like Enid.' The young woman who wrote *Leave Taking* had no idea that a generation who were very young children or who hadn't been born when it was first produced would feel that the play still speaks to their experience. Some of the speeches feel as though they were written recently: Brod's words about having to seek naturalisation after thinking of himself as a British citizen for his whole life echo words spoken thirty years later by victims of the 2018 Windrush scandal.

When I was a child my mother told me that she thought that I might have a gift for clairvoyance. I understand now that she had always instinctively known that I was a writer. It's not that writers are necromancers, but when I read the play I raise again the spirits of those characters. I hear their voices very clearly; I see my younger self consulting with my mother, asking her how you make chocolate tea, and hear her ribbing me all over again about the royalties I owe her or joking that I should credit her as co-writer. I experience again the writing of the scene where Enid breaks down. I know what that feels like now because I have lived through it. I want to ask that young woman if, when she wrote the play, she would ever have imagined that she too would one day howl with grief into a rainy London night after witnessing her mother take her last breath just as Enid howls for a mother she will never hold again.

London, 2018

This is an edited version of Winsome Pinnock's introduction in the 2018 playtext of Leave Taking, *published by Nick Hern Books.*

Introduction

How to use this study guide

This study guide for Winsome Pinnock's *Leave Taking* has been created to provide you with additional material to support your learning of the text. Scenes, characters, context, language, structure and themes are explained in great detail to deepen your understanding. Sample essays and paragraphs, and guidance on how to write an essay, are provided throughout the guide and in a dedicated section. Your task is to combine what you have learned in class with ideas in this study guide by taking part in the writing and research activities to solidify your learning.

Words that appear in **bold** in this guide are explained in keyword boxes in the margin, or in the glossary which starts on page 171. You can also use the glossary to help with revision.

Why *Leave Taking* is such an important play to study

Winsome Pinnock was the first Black British woman to have a play produced at the National Theatre, when *Leave Taking* was revived there in 1995 – making this a monumental play of its time.

The play covers universal themes that were relevant to the audience of the 1980s, but are equally relevant to a contemporary audience watching the play today. It deals with issues around immigration, belonging, parent/child relationships, racism, family and cultural traditions. It is a British play from a Black British perspective and addresses some of the challenges of being Black and British in England in the second half of the twentieth century.

A message from your study guide authors

As two Black British women, we are incredibly excited to see this play added to the programme of study. When we were growing up, there were no plays by Black women on the curriculum for us to study. In this play, Pinnock touches upon so many key issues that are relevant today, and ideas that you will relate to in many ways. It is an accessible play with really rich context and themes. You will get a lot from this guide. So we really hope you enjoy reading and learning, and we wish you all the best in your GCSEs!

Your exam

Leave Taking is a set text on several different exam boards for English Literature GCSE. You might be studying it for an exam set by AQA, OCR or Eduqas.

Assessment Objectives

When your exam paper is marked, whichever exam board you are studying for, the examiners will be looking for four key things. In order to get the highest marks, you have to excel in these 'Assessment Objectives':

AO1	Read, understand and respond to texts. You should be able to:
	• maintain a critical style and develop an informed personal response.
	• use textual references, including quotations, to support and illustrate interpretations.
	The chapters called 'Plot Summary', 'Close Analysis', 'Characters' and 'Themes' will help you with this Assessment Objective.
AO2	Analyse the language, form and structure used by a writer to create meanings and effects, using relevant

	subject terminology where appropriate. *The chapters called 'Close Analysis' and 'Form, Language and Structure' will help you with this Assessment Objective.*
AO3	Show understanding of the relationships between texts and the contexts in which they were written. *The chapter called 'Context' will help you with this Assessment Objective.*
AO4	Use a range of vocabulary and sentence structures for clarity, purpose and effect, with accurate spelling and punctuation. *The chapter called 'Essay Questions and How to Answer Them' will help you with this Assessment Objective.*

My exam board is AQA

Your exam on *Leave Taking* will be called **Paper 2: Modern Texts and Poetry**.

It's a written exam, lasting **2 hours and 15 minutes**.

The paper, which is worth 60% of your whole GCSE, is divided into Sections A, B and C, and only **Section A** is about *Leave Taking*. You should spend 45 minutes on this section.

You have to answer one essay question from a choice of two.

Your essay is worth 34 marks, and they are weighted like this: AO1 (12 marks), AO2 (12 marks), AO3 (6 marks), AO4 (4 marks).

My exam board is Eduqas

Your exam on *Leave Taking* will be called **Component 2: Post-1914 Prose/Drama, 19th Century Prose and Unseen Poetry**.

It's a written exam, lasting **2 hours and 30 minutes**.

The paper, which is worth 60% of your whole GCSE, is divided into Sections A, B and C, and only **Section A** is about *Leave Taking*. You should spend 45 minutes on this section.

You have to answer one essay question and it will be based on an extract from the play, however you have to refer to the whole play in your answer.

Your essay is worth 40 marks, with 5 of the available marks specifically for your writing style (AO4), including your **spelling, punctuation and grammar**. The remaining 35 marks will be awarded for AO1 and AO2.

My exam board is OCR

Your exam on *Leave Taking* will be called **Component 1: Exploring Modern and Literary Heritage Texts**.

It's a written exam, lasting **2 hours**.

The paper, which is worth 50% of your whole GCSE, is divided into Sections A and B, and only **Section A: Modern Prose or Drama** is about *Leave Taking*. You should spend 1 hour and 15 minutes on this section.

You will respond to a **two-part question**:

In **Part a)** you have to **compare an extract** from *Leave Taking* with an extract from another modern drama text that touches on similar themes. You should spend about 45 minutes on this. Your essay is worth 20 marks, and you will be marked on AO1, AO2 and AO3.

AND

In **Part b)** you have to **write an essay** answer to a question which is related in some way – this answer must refer to the whole text. You should spend about 30 minutes on this. Your essay is worth 20 marks, and you will be marked on AO1 and AO2.

Context

Introduction

This chapter focuses on the historical events that have shaped the characters in the play, and the social and cultural experiences in the world of the play when it was written and set. Finally, it explores how the play is still relevant today. Events are explored chronologically for clarity.

There are a variety of exercises that encourage you to consolidate what you have learned, and there are opportunities to do some further reading, and to take in some really interesting video and audio footage, to bolster your understanding of the context.

The colonial Caribbean

Historically, Britain has had a very difficult and complicated relationship with the Caribbean Islands, as part of the former British Empire. The Empire began in the 1500s when Queen Elizabeth I was the head of state. From this period, England ruled over the nations in its Empire, imposing its own laws, religion and culture on the Indigenous people, and often oppressing and brutalising countries into submission.

Between 1640 and 1807, Britain transported an estimated 3.1 million Africans (of whom 2.7 million arrived) on ships to the British colonies in the Caribbean, and North and South America, as slaves. The enslaved people were forced to labour the land in brutal conditions. They were considered property of their owners (who included many British nobles and gentry). The slave trade ended in 1807, but slavery itself was not abolished until 1833. Jamaica gained its emancipation in 1838. The slave owners were compensated for the abolition of slavery, for losses of their human 'property', but the enslaved people were given nothing.

After emancipation, many freed people found ways to build communities by establishing villages and growing their own crops to sell in local markets. Gradually they were able to build their own infrastructure, but the legacy of slavery and plantation life remained: agricultural labour, and the continuation of Christianity which had been enforced on the African peoples by their European oppressors. It is estimated that there are over 1,600 churches in Jamaica – the island has more churches per square mile than any other country.

> *Keyword:* **Mother Country** – The country that possesses or possessed a colony or former colony. For example, under the old British Empire, England was Jamaica's 'Mother Country'.

Eventually, when schools were introduced, the education system was also a way to wield power over the islands, by establishing institutions that would educate Jamaican children within a colonial framework. Students were taught about the kings and queens of England, and were taught using British literature rather than learning to understand their own Jamaican history and culture. This helped to create a hierarchy – a belief that everything British was a pinnacle to be aspired to. Britain was thought of as the '**Mother Country**'. On 24th May, the people of Jamaica would celebrate Empire Day, which was originally to mark the birthday of the reigning monarch – Queen Victoria. It later became a national holiday. This helped to build a bridge between the two countries and foster a sense of belonging.

> Go to this Study Guide's webpage at www.nickhernbooks. co.uk/leave-taking-study-guide-further-resources to find clickable versions of all the links in this chapter and elsewhere.

You can view news articles which describe the festivities of Empire Day through time, here: jamaica-history.weebly. com/may-24th.html

Brod speaks about the impact of Empire Day on his sense of belonging, in Scene Two:

“ BROD. […] All my life I think of meself as a British subject, wave a flag on Empire Day, touch me hat whenever me see a picture a the queen. Then them send me letter say if me don't get me nationality paper in order they going kick me outta the country. (page 27)

In the same scene, Viv indicates her understanding of the direct link between Caribbean people and their African ancestors:

“ BROD. […] These girls got Caribbean souls.

VIV. Don't you mean African souls? (page 29)

> **Writing tasks:**
> - Summarise what you have learned about the colonial Caribbean.
> - How might this context feed into the characterisation of Enid, Mai and Brod? How has this colonial experience shaped them?

The Maroons

Brod refers to Nanny of the Maroons in Scene Two:

66 BROD. [...] When the English fire musket, them bullet bounce off Nanny shoulders kill the men who was trying to destroy her. [...] You, my dear, are descended from Queen Nanny. (page 29)

The Maroons were a group of escaped enslaved people who formed their own settlements and communities in the mountains of Jamaica. They escaped to the mountains for refuge from the English invasion. They developed their own government, culture and traditions (rooted in African traditions) along with their own military to defend against the enslavers. Eventually they formed a treaty with the British, and the Maroons were left to their own devices.

Who was Queen Nanny of the Maroons?

Queen Nanny is an iconic figure for Jamaicans. In 1720 she became the leader of the Maroon community and trained her warriors in guerilla warfare. It is believed that she also practised obeah, to ward off evil spirits. Much of what is known about Queen Nanny has been passed down through **oral** accounts.

> *Key phrase:* **Oral tradition** is when knowledge and culture is received and passed on in spoken (or sung) form, from generation to generation.

You can watch a short video introducing the Maroons and Queen Nanny, here: youtu.be/JblU8scERuw

> **Thinking question:** How does the story of Nanny of the Maroons help you to understand Jamaican culture and pride?

Obeah practices

> *Keyword:*
> **Diaspora** – the dispersion or spread of a people from their original homeland.

Obeah is a religious practice found in African **diasporic** communities, mainly in the Caribbean. It is made up of practices from African religions and spirituality that have survived through slavery and the imposition of Christianity. Obeah involves creating remedies from herbs for illnesses, reading palms, predicting the future, the use of charms for protection or guidance, and offering advice on issues pressing to the individual.

The practice makes ancestral connections to Africa: it is associated with giving reverence to the ancestors and contains elements of the supernatural, animal sacrifices, and divination, with its own set of organised rituals. Practitioners of obeah are known as 'obeah woman' or 'man', and they are believed to have been born with a gift of supernatural powers that have been passed down, or learned from one who has the 'gift' like Mai. They generally cultivate their skills to include herbal remedies, as the practice is often used for healing. Obeah men and women also tend to be intuitive listeners who pay close attention to auras and energies, which helps them to achieve the expected results.

In Jamaica, various Acts of Parliament beginning in 1760 have criminalised obeah, to protect against revolts because its unifying practices provided opportunities for large-scale meetings. Originally punishable by death, later Acts threatened flogging and imprisonment. The law targeted those who honoured and respected the African tradition that connected them to their ancestry. Consequently, it caused a divide between these people and the emerging Black middle classes, who aspired to be like the colonisers, adopting Christian religious values and demonising obeah practices.

In 1998, obeah was decriminalised in Barbados, but it is still an illegal practice in Jamaica.

Writing tasks:

- Write a paragraph explaining how this context helps us to understand Mai's character.
- How might others interact with Mai, based on their knowledge of her participation in obeah?

England's history of migration

There has been a long history of immigration to Great Britain, spanning centuries, and from all over the world. Black communities have been present in Great Britain since the 1500s. 'The dark lady' referred to in Shakespeare's sonnets 127–152 has been speculated to be a Black woman in England at that time, and it is documented that there was a Black presence in England during the Tudor period too: John Blane, for example, was a trumpeter at the court of King Henry VIII. During the late eighteenth century and turn of the nineteenth century, Olaudah Equiano, Ignatius Sancho and Mary Prince wrote about their experiences in slavery and were important in the drive to end slavery as part of the abolitionist movement.

The global history of Great Britain and its relationship with its colonies meant that many people from the colonised countries, including those in the Caribbean, fought alongside the British in both World Wars. Further to this, the Royal Navy was a **catalyst** for Black migration: the demand for manpower encouraged recruitment of Black labour and as a result small Black communities settled around ports such as Bristol, Liverpool and Tilbury Docks in Essex.

> *Keyword:* A **catalyst** is a person or thing that causes an event.

People have at times been able to cross borders freely, however, at various times and increasingly in the past hundred years, migration laws have prevented certain groups of people entering the UK. We will focus on the twentieth century and trace the changes up to how the British Nationality Act of 1981 impacted the characters in the play.

Brod, Enid and Mai would have arrived in England after the Second World War, and likely before the Commonwealth Immigration Act 1968, which reduced the rights of Commonwealth citizens entering the country (see below). In Scene Two, Brod refers to the British Nationality Act of 1981, after which he had to apply for his naturalisation papers.

> *Keyword:* The **Commonwealth** was formed in 1949 to maintain the relationship between the British Empire and its former colonies. Its membership is voluntary, with fifty-six members in 2023. King Charles III is the head of the Commonwealth succeeding Queen Elizabeth II, and remains the official head of state of many of these countries. Barbados is the most recent country to opt out of this arrangement and choose its own head of state.

- **1945–1961**: The 'Windrush' era (see page 19). Post-war growth of Commonwealth immigration, as people from British colonies and former colonies were encouraged to come and help rebuild the country following World War II.

- **1962**: Commonwealth Immigrants Act – this included a system of employment vouchers that restricted entry only to people with a job offer or with skills in short supply. The legislation encouraged people already in the UK to stay, as the law would stop them re-entering if they did leave, and it allowed migrants to bring their families to join them.

- **After 1964**, the new government imposed more restrictions on entry, often using immigration rules. It stopped issuing low-skilled permits, tightened the definition of 'family members' and brought in a tougher standard of proof for family relationships.

- **1968**: The Commonwealth Immigrants Act of 1968 reduced the immigration rights of Commonwealth citizens: only those born or adopted in the UK or who had at least one parent or grandparent born in the UK could enter freely. It was passed in just three days. A little under two months after the 1968 Act passed, Enoch Powell made his 'rivers of blood' speech, calling for 'non-white' immigration to end (read more about this on page 20).

- **1971**: Under the 1971 Immigration Act, a Commonwealth citizen who was not a Citizen of the UK and Colonies (CUKC) would have a 'right of abode' in the United Kingdom after 1st January 1973 only if they were born to or legally adopted by a parent who was a CUKC born in the United Kingdom.

- **January 1973**: Commonwealth citizens who were already in the UK before this date were either entitled to 'right of abode' or held 'deemed leave to remain', but they were not given any documentary proof of their status.

- **1981**: British Nationality Act – in 1981 the Conservative government brought nationality law into line with immigration law. It abolished CUKC status, replacing it with three new categories of citizenship: British citizenship, British Dependent Territories citizenship and British Overseas citizenship. It would have been from this time that Brod had to apply for his naturalisation papers to prove his citizenship and right to stay. Parliamentary records of the time show that applications to register cost £60.

- **In the late 1980s** the government advertised that this time-limited scheme, included in the Nationality Act 1981, to register Commonwealth citizens who had arrived before 1973, was due to expire on 31st December 1987. This is key context for Winsome Pinnock's writing of *Leave Taking*, as the first production of the play opened on 11 November 1987.

The information in this timeline is informed by or taken from pages 55–60 of a government-commissioned independent report called the 'Windrush Lessons Learned Review' by Wendy Williams, published in March 2020.* You can read the full report at assets.publishing.service.gov.uk/government/uploads/system/uploads/attachment_data/file/876336/6.5577_HO_Windrush_Lessons_Learned_Review_LoResFinal.pdf

Windrush generation

Between 1948 and 1973, many Caribbean citizens migrated to England. They are known as the 'Windrush generation', after the *Empire Windrush*, the first ship arriving at Tilbury Docks on 22nd June 1948, carrying 492 migrants. Amongst them were a large number of veterans from the Second World War. Caribbeans were encouraged to come to the UK and assist with the drive to reconstruct following the war: supporting industry and the production of raw material, construction work, and the newly formed NHS. Many sought to contribute and make a better life for themselves.

Suggested extra reading:

Fiction: *Small Island* by Andrea Levy

Non-fiction: *Homecoming: Voices of the Windrush Generation* by Colin Grant

Many migrants took on jobs below their qualification and skills, due to discriminatory attitudes towards Black workers. They were often restricted from applying for certain jobs, which were reserved for British natives, and took on shift work with night shifts. The jobs that the Caribbean settlers took on were essential to the recovery of the country and its economy.

Enid has two jobs, and works seven days a week, partly as a hospital cleaner. In Scene Seven, Brod reveals that he and Enid's husband worked at London's Smithfield meat market.

66 BROD. [...] Them was a good team. I really believe it would work. It wasn't till we get job a Smithfield meat market that him start to change. (page 62)

* Copyright licence: http://nationalarchives.gov.uk/doc/open-government-licence/version/3/

> **Thinking questions:**
>
> *Keyword: A* **monologue** *is a long speech spoken by a single character.*
>
> - How does their hostile working environment impact the characters in the play? Think about Enid, Del and Brod, as well as the experiences of Enid's husband as described by Brod; read Brod's **monologue** in Scene Seven to help inform your answer.
> - How does Pinnock use Brod and Enid's characters as vehicles for exposing the effects of the attitudes of the 1950s on Black Caribbean families?

Many of the migrants at this time were met with hostility. Anxiety and fear amongst the native British about the mixing of cultures and people taking their jobs was widespread.

Enoch Powell's 'Rivers of Blood' speech

By the late 1960s, hundreds of thousands of **Commonwealth** citizens had exercised their legal right to settle in England. The cultural demographic of the country was changing, and labour shortages meant that employers actively recruited immigrant workers, who were cheaper to employ.

Politician Enoch Powell delivered a speech in 1968 appealing to those who opposed immigration. He believed immigration would erode the national character. At the same time, a race relations bill to make it illegal to discriminate on the basis of colour or creed was making its way through parliament. Powell's speech was designed to encourage the prime minister, Ted Heath, to oppose it. The language of Powell's speech incited division, and hate towards Black people:

'We must be mad, literally mad, as a nation to be permitting the annual inflow of some 50,000 dependents [...] It is like watching a nation busily engaged in heaping up its own funeral pyre [...] As I look ahead, I am filled with foreboding; like the Roman, I seem to see "the River Tiber foaming with much blood."'

You can read the full speech here: https://anth1001.files.wordpress.com/2014/04/enoch-powell_speech.pdf

> 💡 **Task:** Read Scene Two, where Brod talks about being British. How does Enoch Powell's speech fuel the attitudes that Brod has towards being British?

It's important to note that, like Enid, the Windrush generation didn't speak very much about their past lives. Some of their experiences might have been very painful. It is, however, well documented that many were very loyal to ideas of Britishness, despite the racism they encountered.

Close-knit communities

Community was integral for the survival of the Caribbean settlers. Many people came over with family or friends from their own islands and also made new connections from different islands on the ship on their way to the UK. Brod and Enid's connection is an example of this close-knit community. Brod clearly has a routine of visiting Enid and her daughters 'for his rice and peas' every day (Scene Seven). When his experience is disrupted, it is a clear sign that Enid is struggling with the loss of her mum:

66 BROD. There was no rice and peas last night, I tell you. You mother gone
     mad. If she din't turn me outta the house. (page 59)

These connections that were forged with people from the Caribbean were fundamental to the growth and development of the community. Some of these relationships were also formed from shared housing situations. This was incredibly common because of how expensive housing was, and also because of a reluctance to rent or sell property to immigrants. This also led the way to what is known as the 'pardner' system in Caribbean communities.

What is a pardner?

A pardner is a system for saving money in a group. The word derives from the word 'partner'. A group of people place an agreed amount of money into a kitty each week or month – each person agrees to contribute the same amount – and at the end of the month, the total sum is given to one member of the group. A rotary system ensures that each individual in the group gets their turn at receiving the lump sum.

This system was essential in supporting Caribbean families to get on the property ladder. Many banks were not prepared to loan or give mortgages to immigrants (especially with low wages), so pardners helped families save for deposits or big purchases (such as a car), or helped generally to support families. A pardner was a verbal agreement and so relied heavily on the trust of the community. Enid refers to community contributions in helping her husband buy his ticket to England:

  66 ENID. [...] Everybody in the district love him, put money down buy him a
       ticket for the ship to England. (Scene Four, page 44)

> Read more about the Windrush generation here, on the British Library website: bl.uk/windrush/articles/how-caribbean-migrants-rebuilt-britain
>
> Watch a three-minute video here about the experience of a Windrush migrant called Rosemarie: youtu.be/3sATGOklv2l
>
> There are more life stories and links to recordings of stories on the British Library website: bl.uk/windrush/articles/windrush-generations-1000-londoners

England in the 1980s

1987 was the year of *Leave Taking*'s first production, and at the time, the play was set in the present. In 1987, the UK's first female prime minister, Margaret Thatcher, was re-elected for the third time. As well as signifying greater than ever female empowerment (a key theme in *Leave Taking*), Thatcher's winning manifesto encouraged a spirit of enterprise. In her eight years in government, unemployment rates had dropped and England seemed more prosperous than ever. Her Conservative government introduced a National Curriculum (in 1988), opportunities to buy homes, better healthcare and better transportation. The gap between the upper classes and working class of society seemed to be closing. All of these changes would imply that life was better.

At the same time, however, industrial workers were staging significant strikes in protest against the Thatcher government's policy of closing and privatising their workplaces; and while some of the working-class group in society were slowly climbing the social scale because of the opportunities provided in employment and education, the aspiration to own their own home and to work their way up the ladder put a lot of pressure on these families, in particular single-parent households, such as Enid's in the play.

Black Britons in government

The geographical spread of the Black Caribbean population across London was changing in the 1980s. There was now a second generation becoming adults who were British-born and felt even more connected to England. This second generation wanted to be more immersed in British society. They fostered political voices and joined political parties. In 1987 the very first MPs from ethnic minorities joined the House of Commons: Bernie Grant, Diane Abbott, Paul Boateng and Keith Vaz.

You can learn more about the first Black parliamentarians here: www.Blackhistorymonth.org.uk/article/section/history-of-politics/the-first-Black-parliamentarians-in-our-times/

Race Today magazine

This magazine was created by British civil rights activists (led by Darcus Howe) along with the Institute of Race Relations, to address the issues that Black Britons faced. You can read an archive of the magazines from 1974 to 1988, online. Take a look at the stories on the front covers to get a sense of what the cultural and political landscape was like: archive.org/details/racetoday

The election of Black MPs was an indication of change in society. The political landscape was adapting to include more ethnic representation. England was becoming more multicultural and this was reflected in the government.

🔆 Thinking questions:

- How does this contextual information about 1987 relate to the characters in the play?
- How might the political landscape have encouraged Viv to study Black Studies at university?
- How might these changes have impacted wider society?

Relationship with the police

In this period, there was a lot of friction between Black people and the police, who had adopted military-style strategies developed by their American counterparts to manage criminality (often targeting young Black men). Discriminatory and unfair policing of Black people resulted in a backlash of riots in pockets of the UK. In 1987, the year in which the play is set, the riot of Chapeltown in Leeds followed the arrest and beating of a Black seventeen-year-old boy, Marcus Skellington.

You can discover more about the Chapeltown riot here: youtu.be/cJdCOjYGEvO

In 1985 the Broadwater Farm riot in Tottenham, London, had erupted after a Black woman, Cynthia Jarrett, died of heart failure during a police raid in her home on the Broadwater estate. Young people took to the streets as a result of this incident, and a Metropolitan police officer, PC Blakelock, was stabbed and killed: horrifically marking a key moment in the fractured relationship between the police and Black communities.

1981 New Cross fire

On the 18th January 1981, in New Cross, London, a fire at a joint birthday celebration for teenagers Yvonne Ruddock and Angela Jackson ultimately claimed the lives of fourteen young people. The area was known for racial attacks and far right political activity, with the National Front, a fascist political party, having a significant presence there. The initial police response was inadequate and slow, and further investigation was inept: no one has ever been held accountable for the deaths of these young people. The community, who suspected an arson attack, came together in protest following the tragedy and marched from Deptford to Hyde Park for Black People's Day of Action on 2nd March that year. Growing tension between the local young Black population and the police over that period finally sparked the Brixton race riots of April 1981, and the riots in Toxteth and Handsworth which followed in July, along with further unrest in a number of other British cities.

> ✎ **Playwright insight:** At the time of the New Cross fire, Winsome Pinnock was studying Drama and English at Goldsmiths' College in New Cross, and she joined the march from Deptford to Hyde Park. Schoolchildren also joined the march, including Pinnock's younger sister.

Watch this TV studio discussion about race and integration in the 1980s: youtu.be/ZKcCGs86M2M

Read more information and watch discussions about the New Cross fire here: Blackhistorystudies.com/resources/resources/the-new-cross-fire/

Del alludes to police discrimination in Scene Two during an argument with Enid. In her attempt to make Enid understand the struggles of the younger generation, she interrogates Enid's perception of how society treats the younger generation:

❝ DEL. But what you give us that we can use out there? You don't see the police vans hunting us down, or the managers who treat us like we're the lowest of the low. You're too busy bowing and scraping to your beloved England. And where's it got you? (page 34)

Sus law

What Del is referring to in this speech is the 'sus' (short for 'suspected person') law – a stop-and-search law that targeted young Black boys in particular during the 1960s to 1980s. It gave police licence to arrest people who they suspected were 'attempting' to carry out a crime. This was very subjective, and it was used by the police to arrest, charge and convict young Black boys and men for minor and in some cases non-crimes. There was animosity and outrage at the misuse of this law and eventually a committee formed called the 'Black People's Organisations Campaign Against Sus' (BPOCAS) who fought to repeal it, and eventually won in 1981. Unfortunately this did not prevent discriminatory arrest. It wasn't until 1999 in the report following the Macpherson inquiry (initiated after the racist murder of Stephen Lawrence) that the police force was officially labelled institutionally racist.

Task: Read 'Sonny's Lettah' by Linton Kwesi Johnson.

You can listen to a musical reading of it here: youtu.be/7uvY5qU7ayg

- What do you learn about the treatment of young Black men?

Keyword:
Unbelonging is a feeling of not belonging in a place, group of people, or culture.

- How might this relate to Del's feelings about the police and her position in society?

- How does this help us to understand the feelings of **unbelonging** in the play? Think particularly about the male characters (those present and those mentioned – Brod, Enid's husband, Mai's son, and Gullyman).

Black youth culture

Keyword: **Assimilate** means to behave in a 'similar' way in order to fit in.

By the 1980s, London was very multicultural. The second generation of Caribbean migrants were mostly **assimilated** into British culture, despite some of the racial inequality. They were carving out their own identity and exploring ways to fit in. Like teenagers today, young people enjoyed socialising with each other, partying, listening to music, exploring fashion, going to the cinema and generally hanging out. Within Caribbean communities there was a history of blues parties, which started in the 1960s as meeting places for Caribbean people. Blues parties, or 'rent parties', were effectively house parties where one would pay a fee to enter the home (which was converted into a club for that evening), and cooked Caribbean food and drinks would be provided. There would be a blend of music from across the decades: 1960s reggae, ska, and later dub, 1970s lovers' rock, and the emerging dancehall music of the later 1980s.

Task: Look up and listen to examples of these different genres of music.

The police would often raid these parties under the suspicion of drug-related activities.

In Scene Two, Del argues with Enid about her night out dancing:

66 DEL. All I did last night was dance. What's wrong with that? I like dancing. I been following that sound system for years. The bass is mad. You wanna see it pounding the walls, like one big pulsing heart. When that bass gets inside you and flings you round the room you can't do nothing to stop it. (page 33)

What were sound systems?

Sound systems originated in Kingston, Jamaica, in the 1940s. They were large speaker systems that were purpose-built to play records to a large-scale audience. They mostly played in downtown Kingston at dancehall parties. They were movable systems that were manned by a selector (like a DJ) who would select the records. An engineer would be responsible for the movement of the equipment and there would also be a security person in charge of looking after it. It would take a whole crew to organise the sound systems. Sound systems became popular in the UK in the 1980s with the evolving set-up of the Notting Hill Carnival. Whilst the main event was carnival, which was itself an opportunity to promote different sound systems and have sound clashes, smaller parties spun off the back of these.

Watch the trailer for the BBC's *Small Axe* here to get a glimpse of youth culture: youtu.be/hrj8HQ6auqs

Watch an interview with director Steve McQueen about the show here: youtu.be/e_41SkKVSTk

You can watch the full episode here: www.bbc.co.uk/iplayer/episode/m000prjp/small-axe-series-1-lovers-rock

Attitudes towards teenage pregnancy

Teenage pregnancies rose significantly in the 1980s, particularly in areas of socio-economic deprivation. Despite there being more family planning facilities and effective birth control measures, teenage pregnancies increased. The reasons behind this are varied: there was more sexual freedom, choice and experimentation, but there were also victims of rape and abuse. Society's discriminatory view on teenage pregnancies was ultimately felt by the young girls in the relationships. There was stigma attached to having children outside of wedlock, which would have been particularly heightened in Christian households like Enid's, which adhered to the belief that sexual intimacy was meant for marriage alone. Society also stereotyped young girls who had babies as 'leeches of the state' – especially young working-class girls, who would be housed under the social care system.

66 DEL. [...] Anyway, I'll be out of here soon. Council put you on the top of the list when you're pregnant. I might get a garden. (Scene Five, page 50)

> *Keyword:*
> **Ostracisation** – the social shunning or shutting-out of a person.

Black, unmarried and pregnant at eighteen, Del would face discrimination and fear **ostracisation** due to Enid's strong religious beliefs. Perhaps this is why she doesn't disclose that she is pregnant to Enid, and also why she moves out. At the same time, Del does not seem too encumbered by these attitudes: she wilfully chooses to have her baby on her own.

Education

Until 1988, teachers were given complete autonomy on what they taught. This led to disparities across the nation, as some students left school without any qualifications at all. The literary texts that were taught were nowhere near as diverse as they are today. It would have been incredibly unlikely that a teenager like Del or Viv would have read a book with any Black characters in it at all – as they discuss in Scene Five (page 53). This lack of representation would have fed into the insecurities of **unbelonging**.

To many Caribbean families, education was a passport to prosperity. It was ultimately the reason that many came to the UK – to offer their children secure futures:

66 ENID. All 'A's. My daughter going to university. How many a my sister children back home going to university? (Scene Two, page 28)

> *Language:* To read more about **patois**, turn to page 142.

> *Keywords:* **Creole** – a language formed from the blending of two or more languages. An **accent** is the way words are pronounced, and differs according to location. **Dialect** is the words used which are specific to a location, such as London, or Jamaica.

Unfortunately this had not always been the case. During the 1970s, a scandalous policy of 'education for the subnormal' that had been in place since 1944 was found to be sending a disproportionate number of Black children to 'ESN' (educationally subnormal) schools – what would today be called 'special' schools. Many mainstream schools felt it a burden to adapt their practices to accommodate this group of migrants and, instead of facing the issue, found it easier to remove them from the classrooms. For many children of migrant families, Standard English was a form of second language, as the language they spoke at home was a Caribbean **patois**, which despite being a form of English had a distinct **accent** and some non-English **creole** words. Some assessments have indicated that **dialect** was a key contributor to the decision to send a child to an ESN school, despite having nothing to do with learning abilities.

While the term 'ESN' was abolished in 1981 and educational inclusivity was enshrined in the law in 1987, Professor David Gillborn, a leading practitioner of critical race studies in the UK, asserts that African Caribbean students in particular had fallen behind the average achievement of their white working-class counterparts in the 1980s.

This context relates to Del's experience of school. It is evident that she has become disaffected and lacks confidence. It is very likely that she has dyslexia which has gone undetected by her teachers, who have labelled her 'slow':

> MAI. [...] The teachers say you slow, so you give up and run with a crowd who make you feel like you belong. (Scene Five, page 47)

Further research:

Read: *Natives: Race and Class in the Ruins of Empire* by Akala

Watch a documentary: Blackhistorymonth.org.uk/article/section/film/subnormal-a-british-scandal/

Twenty-first-century perspectives on the play

Windrush scandal of 2018

The Windrush scandal was a British political scandal that came to media and public attention in April 2018. It was discovered that since as early as 2006, a number of migrants who had arrived in the UK during the Windrush era had been being wrongly detained and even deported.

The 1971 Immigration Act gave anyone who had settled in the UK before 1st January 1973 indefinite leave to remain, but it didn't give them documents to prove it.

People like Brod and Enid in *Leave Taking*, who applied for 'naturalisation papers' between 1981 and 1987, had documents to prove their British nationality and their 'No Time Limit' (NTL) right to live and work in the UK. However, many people did not apply for these papers at that time.

This meant that as immigration laws were tightened in the 2000s, many people without proof of their legal status found that they were unable to access health services, welfare benefits, open bank accounts or get driving licences. Some who left the UK for the first time in decades to visit family found that they were not allowed to return home to England.

When the scandal came to light in 2018, it led to the resignation of the Home Secretary Amber Rudd, a public apology from Prime Minister Theresa May, and the launching of an independent inquiry and 'Lessons Learned' report (you can read this report in full by following the link on page 19). However, by that time, 164 people had been either detained or removed from the UK, or both.

> **Keyword:**
> **Foreshadowing –**
> when a moment in the story hints at something that will happen later.

Even though the play was written and is set in the 1980s, it unknowingly **foreshadows** the events of the Windrush scandal of 2018, as well as touching on the vulnerability of immigrants more generally, because they are subject to swiftly changing immigration laws. All this makes it all the more relevant for a contemporary audience:

66 BROD. [...] All my life I think of meself as a British subject, wave a flag on Empire Day, touch me hat whenever me see a picture a the queen. Then them send me letter say if me don't get me nationality paper in order they going kick me outta the country. You mother, same thing. Ennit, Enid? (Scene Two, page 27)

Read more and watch short clips of Windrush scandal victims Michael Braithwaite and Johnny Samuels speaking about their experiences, here: bbc.co.uk/news/uk-43782241

Feminism

Feminism is advocacy for women's rights, equality and equity. It acknowledges women's strengths, and seeks to empower and acknowledge the experiences of women.

Leave Taking is female-centred, focusing on the experiences of four women across different generations and nationalities. Whilst it does include one male character, it focuses on the lives of Enid, Del, Viv and Mai.

In the epigraph to the published play, Pinnock quotes Alice Walker and Simone de Beauvoir. This helps to set the tone of the play:

'These grandmothers and mothers of ours [were] driven to a numb and bleeding madness by the springs of creativity in them for which there was no release [...] Throwing away this spirituality was their pathetic attempt to lighten the soul to a weight their work-worn, sexually abused bodies could bear.'

Alice Walker, *In Search of Our Mothers' Gardens*

Alice Walker is an African-American writer whose work also centres around the experience of Black women. Her most famous novel, *The Color Purple*, examines the oppressions of Black women in America's Deep South. Her anthology *In Search of Our Mothers' Gardens: Womanist Prose* is a collection of essays, articles, reviews, speeches and statements which reflects her understanding of '**womanist**' theory. It is an ode to women of colour – their strength and survival.

> *Keyword:*
> **Womanist** – a term coined by Alice Walker to describe 'a Black feminist or feminist of colour'.

This quotation refers to the imprisonment of creativity at the hands of slavery. Walker sheds light on the stifling confinement of slavery and labour – it took away space and time to be free, to create, to live, to have joy. The shackles of slavery would not allow people to simply be human. Walker alludes to the paralysis of slavery, which often impacted mental health through generations, even long after the abolition of slavery. This idea is explored in *Leave Taking* through the character of Mooma, and by extension Enid, and her daughters.

Further reading or audio book:

Caste: The Origins of Our Discontents by Isabel Wilkerson

The second quotation in the epigraph is by Simone de Beauvoir:

> '[A mother accepts] a daughter with the bitter pleasure of self-recognition in another victim, and at the same time feels guilty for having brought her into the world.'

Simone de Beauvoir, *The Second Sex*

Simone de Beauvoir was a French philosopher, writer and feminist activist. Her book *The Second Sex* was written in 1949, and discussed the treatment of women at the time and throughout history. In this quotation, de Beauvoir highlights the limitations of patriarchy and the restrictions it places upon women.

> **Task:** Read about the Black feminist movement here: nmaahc.si.edu/ explore/stories/revolutionary-practice-Black-feminisms
>
> - What are the central messages about the position of Black women in society; what do we learn about the struggles and perceptions of Black women?
> - Why do you think it might have been important for Pinnock to centralise the female characters of *Leave Taking*?

The playwright

Winsome Pinnock: biography

Winsome Pinnock is a Black British playwright of Jamaican heritage. When *Leave Taking* was performed at the National Theatre in 1994, Pinnock was the first Black British woman to have a play produced there. She wrote this play at the age of twenty-three whilst she was a member of the Royal Court Theatre's young writers' group. Pinnock realised the lack of diversity in plays being produced at that time. There were very few plays being produced by women or about women, particularly Black women, and she was inspired to write a play that reflected women like her, her family and the people that she knew. Influenced by the feminist groups that she belonged to, she was always informed by the mantra: 'the personal is political', and so her play depicts a domestic everyday setting, but uncovers wider political issues in the fabric of the context, language and form.

> **Playwright insight:**
>
> 'A huge influence on my writing at the time that I wrote *Leave Taking* was the wave of writing by Black women that was coming out of America. Writers like Alice Walker, Toni Cade Bambara and Toni Morrison were incredibly inspiring. I was a young feminist and attended consciousness-raising groups and conferences. My school [in Islington, London] was a base for feminism: the first conference for the second wave of feminism took place there. Many of my teachers were feminist. One teacher in particular introduced more progressive ideas into her teaching. We were shown films and plays that really made you question conventional ideas about gendered roles.
>
> There was a renaissance of Black theatre at the time – in the seventies and eighties. Actor Anton Phillips curated a festival of Black theatre every year, where he would put on plays from around the world. Temba Theatre Company

produced classical plays with all-Black casts. That might be seen as quite radical now! But the female voice was missing. Plays by Black women writers were hardly ever staged, even in Black theatre.'

Inspiration behind the story

Pinnock's characters are in part influenced by people she knew. The character of Enid is influenced by her mother and women like her. Her mother was the source of knowledge for the experience of these women. In a podcast interview with her publisher Nick Hern Books, Pinnock stated that she often would take real life as a starting point for her ideas and take the leap from that into the imagination, making discoveries about her characters as she developed them.

✎ Playwright insight:

'I've never liked writing autobiographically, I've never felt a need to write directly from my life or the life of people I know. I've never been interested in writing about the behaviours of people I know. But as a writer, most of what you do is observing the world around you. Of course, because the writing is from your brain, there are going to be elements of it seeping in, whether you intend it or not.

In the writing of the play, my own mother was a point of research. She had migrated from Jamaica: her and my father came to England in the late fifties and I turned to her to ask her lots of questions on details. There are parts of the play where there are details – for example the reference to chocolate [in Scene Four] is from her. She would tell me some of these practical details. There was a process to make chocolate back home, and this is replicated in the play. It's not in any detail, but I needed to know that. The rest of it [the ideas in the play] is from observation of the world around me.

When I started writing this play, I thought I'd be writing about these two young girls in a way that a twenty-three-year-old might want to: focusing on the new generations. These two young girls were part of a new world, where Black British people were creating this whole new culture. But as I was writing the play, as always happens, my focus shifted. I became more interested in Enid and Mai. I began to feel incredible sympathy for both of them. As I was writing, I had this distinct feeling about the immigrant as an iconic figure – that is true for lots of different cultures. It's not specific to Jamaica and the Caribbean. It's not just about the *Windrush*. That idea of picking up and starting over again in another country is very big. I felt like that was a universal subject that impacts a lot of people.'

'Personal life is inextricable from bigger political issues'

> **Key phrase:**
> **Speaking in tongues** is when people utter speech-like sounds or words of an unknown language during a heightened state as part of religious worship.

British-born and of Jamaican heritage, Pinnock admits that she is caught between two worlds – the Caribbean and England. She is conscious that her people are descended from enslaved people who are disconnected from their original culture and language, and that this is an ongoing legacy of disruption and rupture that has left fragmented histories in its wake. Pinnock came from a spiritual family – going to an Anglican church (where she was not really accepted) and then visiting Pentecostal churches where she witnessed members of the congregation **speaking in tongues**. For her this symbolised a missing language and an attempt to retrieve parts of identity that have been repressed.

Writing is political for Pinnock: she asserts that when you are from an oppressed group of people, picking up a pen to write in spaces where you are underrepresented, invisible, and often silenced, is political. Finding a language for what you want to say (which has never been given a platform) is difficult.

> ✏ **Playwright insight:**
>
> **Keyword: Othering** is the act of treating someone as though they are not part of a group and are in some way different.
>
> 'When women are given the space to write, they sometimes write massive pieces that are complex in their structure, and perhaps that's because they haven't had the opportunity to speak as much and don't know when they will get to speak again. This demonstrates the significance of theatre and opportunities it provides to speak for groups in society that are **othered**. A play is inquiry, investigating the world around you.'

Listen to the podcast interview with Winsome Pinnock, here: soundcloud.com/nickhernbooks/nhbplaygroup-leavetaking-winsomepinnock

> ✏ **Playwright insight:**
>
> 'That message from feminism – that the personal is political – says that the untold stories of women are worth thinking about, writing about. Their lives are historically determined, to some degree.'

> **💡 Task:** *'The personal is political.'*
>
> What does Pinnock mean by this statement? How has this helped to shape her writing of the play? Write at least two paragraphs unpacking this quotation.

What makes the play relevant today?

Pinnock believes that once her plays are written they become their own thing. They are open to interpretation by the audience and directors. She acknowledges that the play changes over time and that the meaning changes with the passing of time. This is because the world around the play changes, and she believes that the context changes the play. Even though the play was first performed in 1987, the core issues and themes of the play are still relevant today. The realism of the play allows for common themes, such as parent and child relationships, coming of age, and migration narratives, to be universal. However, the unique perspective of this being a play about the Black experience of Caribbean migration makes it ever more relevant in the twenty-first century.

The Bush Theatre in London approached Pinnock in 2017 to revive the play, and by the time it was performed there in 2018, the Windrush scandal had blown up in the news, increasing its relevance. Enid's character reflects the hardship that NHS workers suffer today. Issues surrounding migration and acceptance are still ideas that dominate our news. In a lot of ways, the play belongs to any group of people that has not been heard. It speaks for the marginalised groups in society and deals with societal issues, such as immigration and systemic racism, that continue to be relevant.

> **✏️ Playwright insight:**
>
> 'Plays are often of their time, but recently, I did a Q&A for an amateur production and explained that the play was nearly forty years old, and they didn't know. They didn't realise. They thought it was a contemporary play, and that was surprising to me. They said that the relationships shown, they could identify with.
>
> Also, the references about the *Windrush* make it relevant to today. When it was produced at the Bush Theatre, an interviewer thought I had rewritten that section because of the Windrush scandal. I hadn't – that actually happened. I remember my mum having to get her papers in order for the naturalisation process. It's interesting – small events always have a bigger impact. In every play, you're creating a world, so it's like our world and then very different as well.'

Production history

The play premiered in 1987 at the Liverpool Playhouse with the following cast and creative team:

DEL MATTHEWS	Natasha Williams
ENID MATTHEWS	Ellen Thomas
VIV MATTHEWS	Lisa Lewis
MAI	Lucita Lijertwood
BRODERICK	Tommy Eytle

Director	Kate Rowland
Designer	Candida Boyes
Lighting Designer	Les Lyon

The very first production featured some interesting actors. Research them to find out where these stars ended up!

Since that first production, *Leave Taking* has been performed at:

1990: Lyric Studio, Hammersmith, London (in 1991, the play won Pinnock the George Devine Award)
1992: Belgrade Theatre, Coventry
1995: Cottesloe Theatre, National Theatre, London (this auditorium is now called the Dorfman Theatre)
2018: Bush Theatre, London (photographs of this production appear after page 92 in this book)
2022: Tower Theatre, London

Listen to an excerpt of the play recorded in 2010 at the National Theatre Sound Studio: youtu.be/U9fgtbSNwgY

Extra research about the history of Black plays at the National Theatre: artsandculture.google.com/story/Blackplaysatthenationaltheatre/UAVxRuJrcxgA8A

Don't forget: go to this Study Guide's webpage at www.nickhernbooks.co.uk/leave-taking-study-guide-further-resources to find clickable versions of all the links in this chapter and elsewhere.

Plot

This section provides you with an overview of each scene, outlining what happens and how the characters interact. Then there is a chart of the narrative arc, allowing you to explore ideas around the way the play is structured and to what effect. Finally there are some tasks to help you consolidate your learning and to support your revision of the scenes and the characters' development.

Scene One

Who's in it?   Mai, Enid, Del and Viv
Timeline   A Bank Holiday
Set   Mai's Bedsit

Enid visits Mai's bedsit on a Bank Holiday, for an appointment with the obeah woman. Enid's intentions seem to be to gain insight into her sister's request to send money home to Jamaica, and to find out whether her daughter Del is pregnant. This is the first time that Viv and Del have visited Mai's home. Both are intrigued, but Del appears to be unimpressed, whereas Viv is quite inquisitive.

The relationship dynamics between Enid and her daughters are established. Del feels as though she has been brought to Mai's home under duress, and voices this. There is friction between Enid and Del, and Viv's role as a mediator is established.

We learn that Enid left her husband years ago and she has raised the girls alone, and that Del's adolescence is a cause of tension for Enid. We discover that Enid's sister in Jamaica relies on her financially, and that her mother is ill.

The scene ends with a stand-off between Del and Mai. Del insults Mai's obeah practice, calling it 'mumbo-jumbo', and attempts to steal a charm, which Mai calls her out on.

Scene Two

Who's in it?   Viv, Enid, Brod and Del
Timeline   A few days later
Set   Enid's living room

One of the longest scenes in the play, this scene takes place in Enid's home and establishes the roles the characters play in each other's lives. Enid is preparing for a visit from the pastor and seems anxious about his arrival. Viv is in the midst of studying, and Enid interrogates Viv on Del's whereabouts (she has been out all night, and has not been to work).

Broderick, a close family friend, is introduced. He teases Enid about her preparations for the arrival of the pastor and reminisces on shared times back in Jamaica, opening a conversation about feelings of belonging, and British nationality. Broderick feels as though he doesn't belong, and distrusts the British government regarding his right to stay in the UK. Enid, meanwhile, feels as though she has earned her position and afforded her children better opportunities: she brags about Viv going to university. In this scene, we also see the banter and relationship between Brod and Enid, and get a sense of lifelong friendship.

Broderick recalls the story of Gullyman, who attempted to assimilate into his new British 'home' but is a victim of racial attacks that affect his mental health. Broderick informs Viv about the importance of knowing where you come from, and shares a story about Nanny of the Maroons.

Del arrives home and tension rises. Viv and Brod intervene, trying to calm the building conflict, but Enid questions where Del has been, and an argument between the two ensues. Del feels as though she is being treated like a child and Enid is upset at her deception. The argument escalates and the scene ends with Enid slapping Del. Del leaves, and Viv goes after her. Enid then attempts to regain her composure, resuming her preparations for the pastor's visit.

Scene Three

Who's in it?   Enid, Brod and Viv
Timeline   A few hours later
Set   Enid's living room

This scene takes place straight after the pastor's visit. Enid is concerned that she has not made a good impression and is worried that the girls' absence reflects poorly on her. Brod criticises the pastor, stating that he is too arrogant to notice.

Enid is concerned that Del is getting out of hand. Brod questions why Enid worries what people think, why she turns to the church (which he criticises) for support, and why she has finished with the obeah woman. He reminisces about the churches back home and references **'speaking in tongues'**.Then he puts on a record and they share a dance.

Viv returns tentatively. The phone rings and it is Enid's sister Cynthia calling from back home. Whilst Enid takes the phone call, Viv discusses her desire to go to Jamaica with Brod. Enid interjects whilst on the phone to her sister, assuring Viv that she doesn't understand the levels of poverty back home and that she must not be fooled by images of paradise.

Enid's phone call continues, and it is revealed that her mother, Mooma, has died in Jamaica, marking a turning point in the play. Enid is in denial at first and suspects that her sister wants money, then accuses her family of having killed Mooma. However, Brod assures her that her mother very likely died of old age, and the scene ends with her going offstage to make arrangements to send money.

Scene Four

Who's in it?   Viv and Enid
Timeline   Late that night
Set   Enid's living room

Enid is sitting on the sofa in the dark sipping a drink when Viv enters. Enid reflects on her life back home in Jamaica and shares the hardship that she suffered. She talks about the hunger, hard labour and poverty that she endured. She bitterly reflects on the fun that people made of her and her family. Enid speaks about an uncle and the lasting impression he and his wife made on her, creating a desire for her to go to America. This is the first time that Viv gets a deeper insight into her mother and her upbringing.

Enid shares memories of Mooma making chocolate tea, taking her on a long walk, and singing a song which Enid sings a little of for Viv. Enid recalls the day she left Jamaica, and we gain an insight into Enid's relationship with her mother and the lack of love she felt. This is a nostalgic scene that reflects memories of her life back home.

Enid also tells Viv about the girls' father (whom she does not speak about generally) and recalls their early memories together, when they would sit and plan their future. She tells Viv he was charming and admired by many. He was a big

Context: Turn to page 21 for contextual information about financial struggles for Black immigrants to the UK.

dreamer and ensured that he fulfilled his dream to move to England and send for her. Then she shifts the conversation's focus to a donation that she has been saving for Viv to support her at university. She insists that Viv takes the money and the scene ends with Enid declaring that she wants to go home.

Scene Five

Who's in it?   Del, Mai and Viv
Timeline   A few weeks later
Set   Mai's bedsit

Del, who is pregnant as Enid had suspected, has moved in with Mai, staying in her estranged son's bedroom. They seem to have adapted to each other comfortably and Del asks Mai a lot of questions about her life. Del starts to learn about obeah practices, maintaining a degree of scepticism and joking that Mai is making it up.

Mai reads Del's palm, leaving Del surprised and assured of Mai's knowledge. They joke about Del overstaying her welcome and causing disruption in Mai's home, but have clearly come to a comfortable arrangement. Mai exits as Viv enters.

The visit is unexpected. Viv has come to petition for Del to leave: she has heard from the father of Del's baby, who is begging to see her. Del does not seem to care, and does not want to see him. Viv offers Del the money that Enid has given her, believing that she will be in more need of it, raising a child on her own.

Viv shares how disconnected she feels from education, feeling that she cannot identify with the ideas taught and that her teachers do not understand her. Del berates Viv for walking out of her English exam and the scene ends with Del kicking Viv out, telling her not to return until she completes her examinations.

Scene Six

Who's in it?   Mai, Enid and Del
Timeline   A few weeks later
Set   Mai's bedsit

Enid has visited Mai for another reading. The scene begins with the end of the appointment. Enid is clearly distracted and weary. She offloads onto Mai that she is worried about Del, and informs Mai that Del has run away from home and she has not seen her in weeks. Mai reassures her that Del will be all right. Enid questions her own parenting and doubts whether she has been a good mother. She worries that she has let Del down and that Del will destroy her own life. She recalls the shame of an incident where Del was arrested for shoplifting.

Enid discloses that she hasn't slept and feels guilty for not sending more money back home, blaming herself for Mooma's death. They discuss the choices they made to leave Jamaica for the betterment of their children. Enid talks about the struggles of being a single parent. Mai gives Enid something to help her sleep, and Enid leaves.

Del enters Mai's room to let her know she is going for a walk. Mai expresses how tired she is of obeah and tells Del that she is finished with it. Mai feels guilty and tells Del to leave. Del protests, insisting that Enid hates her. Mai shares that she feels being too hard on her son drove a wedge between them and insists Del should make amends with Enid. The scene ends with Del leaving to go for a walk.

Scene Seven

Who's in it?   Mai, Del and Brod
Timeline   Very early the next morning
Set   Mai's bedsit

The scene opens with Broderick splayed out on the dining-room table, apparently dead but actually drunk from the night before. Del has obviously allowed him in, and Mai asks who this man in her living room is.

Broderick informs them both that Enid has thrown him and Viv out of the house. This scene focuses heavily on Broderick. We learn that he had his own family and that it broke down because of the mistakes he made in the past. He delivers a **monologue** about Enid and her relationship with the girls' father. He informs Del that her father was a good man who faced many challenges resulting in changed behaviour. A theme of emasculation linked to racism unfolds. Brod alludes to the idea that there was domestic violence and Del interrupts him, stating that she does not want to hear any more. He explains that Enid wanted to bring the children up in a healthy environment, which is why she left her husband. Brod tries to humanise Enid to Del, and when he leaves, Del releases her pent-up feelings, kicking the wall. The scene ends as Mai notices traits in Del's face that indicate that she may share the gift of obeah.

Scene Eight

Who's in it?   Del, Mai and Enid
Timeline   A few weeks later
Set   Mai's bedsit

The scene opens with Del calling upon a goddess for money and prosperity. Mai chastises Del for using Mai's equipment for her own selfish gains. Del has cleaned the room and attended to one of Mai's clients. Mai warns Del to keep the obeah practices that occur in her home private. We see that they have developed a bond.

Del detects that Mai may have some health complications, after reading her palm, and tells her that she should go and see a doctor. Mai avoids the conversation, but a new understanding of each other is reached. Del also realises that a lot of what Enid feels – alienation and isolation – is a shared experience across generations.

Mai dupes Del into having an appointment with Enid. Del informs Enid that Broderick told her about her father, and asks why she keeps so many secrets. Del gives Enid back the money, insisting that it's needed back home. Enid tells her that Viv is getting ready to go to university to read Black Studies.

Del questions Enid's love for her, and Enid shares her childhood experiences of feeling disliked by her own mother. She acknowledges that she is aware of the way Del is treated and that she would do anything for her children. She has fought to get them to this point, and she is tired. This is the beginning of the repair of their relationship. She now needs somebody to love and look out for her. The play ends with Del taking and smoothing her mother's hand for a palm reading.

A note on structure

Most narratives follow this simple structure of a narrative arc:

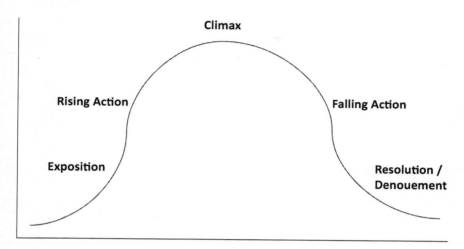

Exposition	Scene One
	When the four central characters are introduced and the relationship dynamics between Enid, Del and Viv are established.
Rising Action	**Scene Two**
	At the end of Scene Two, when the argument between Enid and Del escalates, and culminates in a slap.
Climax	**Scene Three**
	When Enid receives a phone call from Cynthia informing her that Mooma has died.

Falling Action	Scene Six
	When Enid visits Mai for a second time to get a reading, and confides that she is feeling the weight of Mooma's death.
Resolution	Scene Eight
	When Enid visits Mai for a reading and Mai orchestrates a resolution between Enid and Del.

Activities and thinking questions

- How does Pinnock structure the play to retain the interest of the audience or reader?
- Identify the moments of flashback in the play – how do these help to inform our ideas about the characters?
- Track Enid's journey through the play – can you identify the turning point for her? How is it marked?
- Can you identify the key moments of tension? How are these moments marked?
- Mark the moments when we last see each character – what is significant about their departure from the play?

Turn to page 139 for a more detailed exploration of the structure of the play.

Close Analysis

In this section, we are going to explore each scene in greater depth. This will enable us to build up a detailed understanding of the characters as they develop, as well as homing in on powerful quotations to aid with responding to exam questions. We will also track how themes emerge and how they relate to the characters, as well as the context of the story Pinnock is conveying to her audience.

We will analyse the play scene by scene using the following structure to guide us through:

1. Setting
2. Key points to consider
3. Key characters and what we learn
4. Task(s)
5. Model paragraph
6. Writing task – you try it!
7. Context and emerging themes
8. Language

Scene One

Setting

❝ MAI's *bedsit. Very messy* [...] (page 13)

The opening **stage directions** are quite precise and detailed. We are given enough information about Mai's bedsit to imagine or to recreate it as a director.

> Keyword: **Stage directions** are written into playtexts to tell the director and actors what should happen physically on stage.

Although a bedsit is usually just one room, it may be that Mai has a separate kitchen space or a shared kitchen, as the stage directions indicate that the kitchen is offstage. We learn that Mai has to share the bathroom with the landlady.

Keyword: **Props** are objects used on stage by actors.

What **props** and furniture would you need to create this scene? Examine the **stage directions**. What else might you add, and why?

Context: Turn to page 16 for contextual information about **obeah**.

Context: Turn to page 142 for detail about Jamaican **patois**.

Context: Turn to page 19 for contextual information about the **Windrush generation**.

Key points to consider

- Introduction of Mai's bedsit as a key location throughout the play.
- Introduction of spirituality through obeah.
- Introduction of Jamaican patois/**dialect** through both Mai and Enid.
- Del and Viv are defined as British-born and speak with London **accents**, with some influence from their Jamaican culture.
- Del and Viv's initial alienation from the strange practice of obeah, their surroundings, and Mai.
- The contrast in temperament and character of Viv and Del.
- The two generations – Windrush generation immigrants versus second-generation, Black British people.
- That Enid is a single parent.
- The responsibilities of having to provide for family back in the Caribbean.
- Del's attitude towards Mai.
- The introduction of ideas about identity.
- Form: two conversations taking place on stage at the same time.
- Friction between Enid and Del.
- The start of Del and Mai's relationship.

Key characters and what we learn

Mai

We learn that Mai is a significant character in her community and known as an obeah woman. She presents as old, with failing sight and possible arthritis. Her dwelling is extremely humble, 'messy' and cluttered. It is possible that 'bedsit' means that she lives with other tenants and certainly the landlady is also in residence. She seems nervous of upsetting the landlady, which might indicate that her tenancy is not a secure one, so she doesn't live freely.

Mai makes several references to life in the UK compared to 'home', including how her profession has a different focus in the UK, as shown by the phrase 'over here':

66 MAI. [...] Plenty black woman over here does come see me
      'bout man. (page 17)

Mai refuses to get drawn into family tensions and realises that the best course is to offer straightforward advice with regards to Enid's family abroad and her need to delve into Del's life:

66 MAI. [...] Take my advice: leave her to do what she want and
      get yourself a good night's sleep. That's what I would do.
      (page 20)

At the end of the scene, Mai cuts through Del's rudeness and hostility and reaches out to her, **foreshadowing** their relationship later in the play:

66 MAI. Anytime you need someone to talk to, I'm always here.
      (page 23)

> *Keyword:*
> **Foreshadowing –**
> when a moment in
> the story hints at
> something that will
> happen later.

Del

Del is Enid's eldest daughter, at eighteen, and has already left school. Our first impression is of a sullen girl, underwhelmed by everything and somewhat irritated at, and beleaguered by, her

> Keywords:
> **Exaggeration** and **hyperbole** are English and Greek words meaning almost the same thing – but 'hyperbole' is particularly used when writing about literary technique: it means 'exaggeration used for effect'.

mother. She responds negatively to Mai and her surroundings, describing the place as a 'mess'. She is annoyed with Enid for engaging in this practice, referring to it as 'mumbo-jumbo'.

However, it is clear that her reaction of disgust is **exaggerated** as she is keen to rummage through Mai's possessions: feigning disinterest, but absorbing Viv's explanations. Whilst she expounds scepticism, it is dramatic when she breaks off Mai's reading:

66 MAI *takes* DEL's *palm, looks at it then looks into* DEL's *eyes, then down at her palm again* [...] DEL *drags her hand away.* (page 22)

She steals a charm from Mai and deliberately hangs back as they leave. This tells us that she has a sense that maybe Mai can read her soul, and in some way she is moved, and curious enough to steal.

Viv

Viv, who is seventeen, is presented as more open and agreeable. She requests that her obeah reading focuses on whether she will be successful in her exams.

She too is alarmed by the surroundings, but her curiosity grows as she and Del explore the room and the obeah paraphernalia. Viv relates what they see back to Broderick's teachings. The theme of identity and belonging emerges through Viv's need to understand her Jamaican heritage:

66 VIV. [...] Uncle Brod says you don't know who you are 'less you've been there. (page 20)

Viv's role as mediator between Enid and Del is established. We can see that Viv has a more positive relationship with her mother.

Enid

Enid seems to be under a lot of stress, and her visit to Mai is in earnest. She is worried about being manipulated by her sister into sending money back to Jamaica to help her 'sick' mother. She is also concerned about Del and her change in attitude.

> 66 ENID. She never used to be like this. All on a sudden she change, won't listen to me any more. Angry. Like she possessed. (page 20)

Why do you think there might have been a 'sudden' change in Del's behaviour?

It seems that obeah is an important part of her life that Enid has avoided but needs to reconnect with in order to find peace. She clearly wants to include the girls, knowing that they are at crucial moments in their lives, and as we later learn, it's a rare occasion when Enid actively connects them with a key aspect of their heritage.

Character tracker

Complete this table for each scene to track what you have learned about the characters. Here it is with just two characters filled in as an example:

	Mai	Enid
Notes	Has noticed the changes in practising obeah in Jamaica versus the UK. Is menaced by her landlady. Tries to recreate back home with chickens in the backyard. Is keen to stay out of family squabbles.	Is a single parent. Feels pressures from family abroad. Is worried about her daughters. Turns to Jamaican cultural practices to help with life in the UK. Has friction with her eldest daughter.

	Mai	Enid
Key quotations	'I don't deal in numbers. Is people I deal in.' (page 14) 'Is a free country, ennit? I couldn't live without a few fowl in the backyard.' (page 21)	'Thas why I come here. For you to help me. Please read the big one first.' (page 21)
Adjectives, feelings	Friendly, suspicious, wise, calm, measured	Worried, anxious, infuriated, perplexed, maternal

Task

Asking yourself questions about the characters and what your first impressions are is a good way of keeping track. Choose a character to write about, pulling together what you have learned. Always use quotations to support your ideas.

Model paragraph

> ### What do we learn about Mai in Scene One?
>
> When we first encounter Mai in Scene One, she appears a bit muddled and possibly even dishonest in her practice. When she says: 'You must be speak to me secretary' (page 14) it is a clear comic moment for the audience, as this business language is out of keeping with the 'very messy' (page 13) surroundings and it is obviously untrue. However, Pinnock changes the audience's perspective over the course of the scene. At the end, Mai turns her attention to Del and says, 'Anytime you need someone to talk to, I'm always here' (page 23), sensing that Del is the most in need. Her offer

foreshadows the fact that we will see their relationship develop later in the play. She is also portrayed as observant, insightful, or even mystical, outwitting Del with the challenge: 'And I know your game... (*Holds her hand out.*) The charm please' (page 24). Her commanding language here is very assured, so that by the end of the scene the audience has much greater respect for her than at first impression.

Writing task – you try it!

What impressions do you gain from Scene One about Enid's relationship with Del?

Think about:

- Why Enid goes to Mai and brings the girls.
- Exchanges between Del and Enid.
- What Mai says about their relationship.
- Contrasts between Viv and Del.

Use quotations and, if it helps, you can use a **PEAL** structure – make a **P**oint, use a quotation (your **E**vidence), and explain how this relates to your point by **A**nalysing the language in the quotation, and then **L**inking to your next point.

Context and emerging themes

We are introduced to obeah and two of the three Windrush generation characters. The theme of heritage and identity is raised (we see how Mai continues her obeah practice). We also see how having extended family abroad creates pressures. The same themes arise through Del and Viv, representing the younger British-born generation. They are unfamiliar with obeah, though Viv has a cursory understanding via Brod and an emerging need to know about where she is from. The setting is presented to us the audience and to the girls as foreign, but also as an aspect of London life for some older Caribbeans.

> For more on this topic turn to the chapter on Themes, from page 119.

Language

Turn to page 142 to read more about the two distinct **dialects** in the play.

Pinnock sets the tone of the play by introducing us to two modes of communication – the **1980s London dialect** of the girls and the **Jamaican patois** of Mai and Enid. We get the impression that Del and Viv are familiar and comfortable with this too. Enid speaks to them in patois but it is not how they speak to her. Del gently mocks their surroundings by referring to 'duppies and rolling calves': ideas that British-born Caribbeans might hear talk of throughout their childhoods.

> **'Duppies and rolling calves'**
>
> Duppy is the term used for ghosts and evil spirits in Jamaican folklore. The rolling calf is seen as the spirit of a dead person returning to haunt villages and seek revenge.

Keyword: **Rhetorical questions** are questions that do not expect an answer but are instead intended to make the listener think about what the answer would be. They are a very persuasive and impactful literary technique.

We notice that the Jamaican patois **dialect** omits words in sentences, and that Mai tells quick, efficient stories in brief but descriptive sentences, ending with a **rhetorical question** or an observation. The story of why she no longer offers healing baths ends with:

66 MAI. [...] How she going catch anything when all my clients much cleaner than she? (page 17)

The **dialect** is accessible but builds up a picture of another culture. We are introduced to words such as 'unno' which means 'you' or 'you all'. Del also uses the phrase 'Don't touch the woman's things'. There is a link here to a mantra of the older generation who say 'don't touch people tings' or 'leave the people dem tings'. Perhaps Del is gently mimicking, or perhaps this is an unconscious habit as this idea would be ingrained in her culture and upbringing.

Keywords: **Contrast** is used for effect by writers, to emphasise the differences between people, places or things. It is also an effective technique to draw contrasts in your own essays.

The dual conversations between Del and Viv and then Mai and Enid allow the **contrast** of the two generations' use of language to be observed simultaneously, so we see how the modes of communication meet and divide.

Scene Two

Setting

This scene establishes the other main setting in the play. The living room is multifunctional: where the pastor will be entertained as well as where much of the conflict and the family revelations take place. There is a **contrast** with Mai's bedsit: Enid's home is orderly and comfortable.

Key points to consider

- Broderick provides humour in this scene, as well as the only male voice.

- He provides insights into Enid's character before coming to the UK.

- Broderick also introduces the first explicit discord in the play about life in the UK.

- The scene highlights the **contrast** in the relationships Enid has with each of her daughters.

- We see the relationship between Brod and Viv.

- Mental health and the impact of racism are explored through the story of Gullyman.

Key characters and what we learn

Viv

In many ways, Viv is the peacemaker. She enjoys an easy relationship with Enid and they share a quiet and humorous moment at the beginning of the scene.

It is clear that the anxiety expressed in Scene One is rising as her exams loom:

66 VIV. And what if I fail my exams? What'll she do then?
(page 31)

Viv wants to please her mum, but is beginning to have aspirations outside of her mother's expectations.

Del

Pinnock brings the tensions detected in Scene One to a climax as the scene ends with Del leaving. Del's anger and frustration are expressed:

66 DEL. Grateful for what? This shithole? A greasy job in a greasy café where they treat me like a dum dum [...] ? (page 34)

This conveys how undervalued Del feels in society, both in her experience of school and at work. She is angry as Enid seems unable to acknowledge or understand this. In the story she relates about Enid, Del outlines the racism:

66 DEL. [...] And, in front of everyone, matron tells you to clean it up. (page 34)

Keyword: **Tone** is the way in which a writer or speaker conveys their attitude to what they are saying.

Del is trying to draw a parallel with her own experiences so that Enid can see. Del follows up with: 'Yes, England loves you, all right,' and in her **tone** of sarcasm we can see the pain and burden of prejudice and racism. This memory is traumatising for Del, as she pictures her mother being humiliated, and she compares this to her everyday interactions with her boss.

🖊 **Playwright insight:**

'When Del describes her mum having to go and fetch the mop and bucket, that is one moment in the play that is autobiographical. It happened at a party in a hospital where my mother worked. I did witness that, and it still makes me feel incredibly emotional.'

Broderick

Broderick is presented as a friend of the family (it was common for Caribbean children to refer to close family friends as 'Uncle' and 'Aunty' as in Scene One), and we already know from Viv that he enjoys schooling the girls and sharing knowledge from 'back home'. He enters in a jovial way, a welcomed part of the family, and his easy banter with Enid is affectionate and injects Caribbean humour and **dialect** into the scene:

66 BROD. [...] The smell a bleach frighten off every duppy from here to the Elephant and Castle. (page 26)

We see many sides to his character, including the fun and playful, the brooding and reflective, as well as his role as a father-figure and teacher. It's important to Brod that the girls know that they have 'Caribbean souls' (page 29) and the conflict between British and Caribbean culture is developed further in this scene.

Broderick also introduces Gullyman and the impact of racism on mental health and wellbeing.

> ✏ **Playwright insight:**
>
> 'As a child I knew of a few women who suffered with mental health issues. It was understandable − their families were breaking up. My mother would invite them to our house. We didn't have much, but we would share what we had. Mum would feed them, talk to them. There was one woman who came every single week. As time went on, she spoke less and less because she was so ill. We didn't tend to speak or write about these things, but there was an untold pressure on Black people that impacted their lives greatly.'

Broderick relates his experience of the **Windrush scandal** and how it has influenced his sense of identity:

66 BROD. Call me a alien. As if me live the last thirty years on the moon instead of on this blasted estate. (page 27)

Context: Turn to page 29 for contextual information about the **Windrush scandal**.

He picks up on the extreme **othering** effect of the legal term 'alien', and it is clear from his **tone** of outrage that he doesn't feel welcomed. We learn that the stories and history he relates keep him connected to Jamaica.

Enid

Enid shows us her Christian side in this scene, contrasted with the Jamaican spirituality of the obeah she seeks out in Scene One. Here we see her preparing for the pastor's visit, while still fretting about Del.

She is in a good mood and we see a gentler, lighter side to her, and how proud she is, in her exchange with Viv. Enid counters Brod's warnings about being too English, defiantly asserting:

66 ENID. [...] I proud a my English girls. (page 29)

What is revealed is that she approves of Viv's pathway but rejects Del's form of 'Englishness'. Whilst she believes that the girls are English and that she has earned her citizenship, the scene ends with her asserting her Jamaican identity in order to cope and make sense of Del's behaviour:

66 ENID. People grow up in England think they can talk to you anyhow. Well they can't. (page 35)

Enid shows here the challenges of the generational divide living across two cultures. Enid wants to **assimilate** into British society, but holds on to her morals and values shaped in Jamaica.

Task

Broderick is the only male character, and we learn a lot about him in this scene. Make a table of points with supporting quotations, about Brod as a father figure, a teacher, his humour and how he feels about life (what he has seen and experienced).

Brod the father figure	Brod the teacher	Brod and his humour	Brod on life

Model paragraph

> **How does Pinnock build tension in this scene towards the final showdown between Del and Enid?**

Pinnock creates tension in this scene by building on clues given in Scene One, such as Enid not being happy with the decisions Del is making. Scene Two opens with Enid and Viv in an exchange that shows their rapport and affection for each other. The aspects of Viv's character that Enid feels are lacking in Del are highlighted as she draws on her education to make a joke by quoting Shakespeare: 'Out, out damned spot' (page 24). The **contrast** with Del is then highlighted when Enid immediately asks, 'How come I never hear Del come in last night?' (page 25). Viv tries to cover for her sister, but senses that neither Del nor Enid will back down. She pleads, 'Promise me you're not going to make a scene' (page 25) as Pinnock **foreshadows** that a breaking point is imminent.

Writing task – you try it!

How do identity, generational differences and location of birth become negative forces in Scene Two?

Write about:

- Brod and how he feels stripped of his identity.
- Gullyman and the significance of his story.

- Del's frustrations.
- How Viv sees herself.
- Tensions between Del and Enid.

Context and emerging themes

Broderick references the impact of immigration legislation on his sense of belonging. We also see how racism and feeling outside of mainstream society affects each of the characters and other people they know. Broderick explores how it can affect a person's mind through the story of Gullyman. The contrast with the effect on the younger generation is also explored, mainly through Del pushing back against her mother's approach of playing by the rules.

Identity and how it shifts through the scene is very effective and draws the audience into the sense of confusion the characters feel. Viv uses English poetry to define and reinforce her Britishness as she recites, '"A dust whom England bore, shaped, made aware…"' (page 30), however when Brod raises the possibility of being kicked 'outta the country', Viv asks 'Where would me and Del go?' (page 27).

Enid, too, displays an ambivalent sense of her belonging, through conforming but not really embracing the way that young people are in the UK. She clings to her own traditions, and is outraged and unimpressed with Del's behaviour.

Language

As in Scene One, Pinnock uses **patois** and **London dialect** to contrast the generations and further develop the characters' thoughts and feelings.

Although this is a very dramatic scene, language is used to highlight the Caribbean sense of **humour**, as Brod teases Enid about her 'crack foot-bottom' (page 27). The banter between Enid and Brod is edgy and direct but largely friendly, with Enid alluding to Brod's love of drink as she cleans the carpet:

66 ENID. This is a map a your life, Brod: wine stain, Guinness, brandy... (page 26)

Language is also used to imply past events, and we see Enid using a sarcastic **tone** levelled at Broderick:

66 ENID (*pointed*). No, it doesn't bother some man, does it, Brod? (page 32)

Enid's **subtext** seems to be pointing to Brod's marital breakdown or his attitude to women and relationships.

In this scene, Pinnock also uses **storytelling** as a device to introduce other characters and themes, by succinctly relating an idea or lesson to the audience. This storytelling tool is used by Del and Brod to cover many subjects within the scene:

1. Immigration – Brod

2. Racism (as experienced by Gullyman) – Brod

3. A night out in 1980s London – Del

4. Enid's experience of workplace racism – Del

5. Jamaican history: Nanny of the Maroons – Brod

6. Enid's life in Jamaica – Brod

This way of conveying life's meanings through stories is popular in the Caribbean. Pinnock uses language to reach inside the stories the characters are telling and quickly bring out the mood and feeling by carefully selecting impactful statements: for example when Del recounts, 'The bass is mad [...] When that bass gets inside you and flings you round the room you can't do nothing to stop it' (page 33) she uses **imagery** to sum up why this experience is more engaging than her work life. Del's approach echoes Brod, and perhaps she has learned this way of speaking from him. Pinnock shows how the generations seamlessly merge as well as diverge through language.

> *Keyword:* **Subtext** means information which is suggested by the words on the page, without being said directly.

> *Context:* To read more about the device of **storytelling** as it is used in the play and in Caribbean **oral tradition**, turn to page 111.

> *Keywords:* **Imagery** is when writers use language to paint pictures in the audience's mind. **Metaphors** and **similes** are examples of imagery, as is **personification**, when something non-human is written about as if it has human characteristics.

Scene Three

Setting

> 66 *A few hours later. Late evening.* ENID *is tidying up.* BROD *sits on the sofa, loosening his tie.* ENID *hums 'Nothing but the Blood of Jesus' as she clears up.* BROD *takes a surreptitious swig from his flask then tucks into the leftover nibbles, contributing the odd line to the hymn.* (page 35)

The pastor's visit has taken place and much of the tension of Scene Two seems to be lifted.

Key points to consider

- How the tension in Scene Two is contrasted with the relative calm of this scene in its opening, but then it develops into heightened drama and a death.

- Viv is beginning to assert her own needs and personality by challenging Enid's goals for her.

- We see the contrast in how Brod and Enid view religion and its significance in the UK and Jamaica. Brod presents the idea that religion promotes unity and authenticity 'back home', compared with an obsession with being respectable and conforming in its UK version.

- Enid's doubts expressed in Scene One about the constant requests for money return to haunt her in the death of Mooma. We see Mai's advice proven right and the pastor's blessing of the house to be futile.

Key characters and what we learn

Enid

In this scene, we discover that Enid is keen to belong, fit in and be respected:

66 ENID. He's a high man. It look bad that Viv and Del wasn't
    here? (page 35)

She wants the approval of the pastor, craving validation, and
Broderick deflects this with a joke, without being unkind.

Enid blames Broderick for Viv's desire to visit Jamaica:

66 ENID. [...] You see what nonsense you put in the girl head?
    (page 39)

Enid only sees Viv through the aspirations she has for her, and
cannot fathom that Viv too is looking for meaning and a sense of
her identity and roots. The word 'nonsense' is dismissive in **tone**
but the phone call interrupts any potential conflict, and we see how
unprepared Enid is for what happens.

We are shown the stark realities of having ties abroad and what can
happen:

66   As ENID *listens something drains out of her. She drops the
     phone* [...] (page 40)

Pinnock shows us how the distance to family abroad is impactful
when disaster occurs. We see the resolution of Enid's conversation
with Mai in Scene One as, without question, she makes immediate
plans to send financial assistance.

Broderick

Brod's role in the family is further cemented in this scene. It is clear
that he has a different view of the UK to Enid, and that view
extends to having more empathy with the younger generation:

Context: Turn to
page 24 to read
about rioting in this
period.

66 BROD. Rude? You seen them kids rioting on TV? Thas what
    you call rude. [...] Those girls ain't wild, Enid. (page 36)

Brod recognises that the girls' pushback is linked to the unrest amongst Black youth depicted on TV. We see Broderick stepping in as the scene ends, to support Enid, and whilst she chides him for 'taking sides', it is clear that he is an integral part of Enid's support system.

Viv

Viv asserts herself for the first time in this scene. She dares to share her own aspirations and incur Enid's wrath:

66 VIV. I been thinking about Jamaica. [...] Loads a people take a year off. (pages 38–39)

We can see how Brod's cumulative stories have impacted Viv, and she realises that if Enid will not share and be open about their roots, then it is possible to assert her independence by travelling to make her own connections to them.

Tasks

1. 'In this scene, Enid begins to question her attachment to obeah and chooses religion as perhaps another step to acceptance in the UK.' Do you agree?

2. Make two lists: of Enid's views of obeah in Scene One, and in Scene Three.

3. Collect quotations on Brod's view of religion from pages 36 and 37.

4. How does Brod's view differ from Enid's?

Model paragraph

> ### Why is the Pastor's visit important to Enid?
>
> It is clear through Scenes One and Two that Enid wants to be accepted and respected, along with her family. We know from her visit to Mai that she is also seeking spiritual guidance, so in Scene Two she goes to great effort to impress the pastor ahead of his visit. After his visit, in Scene Three, she reflects, 'I feel so shame when Pastor ask me where them was. You think him know me was lying?' (page 36) Her use of the word 'shame' makes clear that Enid cares deeply about how she is perceived by him. Her 'lying' **contrasts** with the more open approach she takes with Mai in Scene One, as she feels a need to show the pastor that she is leading a moral Christian life. We know from Scene Two that Enid wants to fit in and follow the rules, and her rejection of obeah in this scene: 'Me finish with obeah woman' (page 36) shows that she thinks Christianity is a better choice. As part of her drive to **assimilate**, Enid seems to be trying to cut ties with the parts of her culture that are not seen as respectable in the UK.

Writing task – you try it!

What do we learn about Viv in this scene?

Think about:

- Her role as peacemaker.
- Her academic success.
- How she sees herself.
- Why she might want to go to Jamaica.
- Her standing up to Enid.

Context and emerging themes

Read over the sections in the Context chapter on pages 14 and 16 about religion.

Also read about Enid's religion in particular on page 97.

You can also read in the Themes chapter about pressures on immigrants with families abroad, and the families they built in England (page 126).

Language

Many aspects of Jamaican **patois** emerge as this scene focuses on just Brod and Enid. This demonstrates how language shifts, moderates and deepens, depending on who is part of the conversation. Enid and Broderick are close friends and know each other from 'back home', and therefore more unfamiliar words and phrases are packed into their dialogue. We see Broderick referring to Enid as 'Miss Enid' – a custom used widely in the Caribbean to show respect. He does this after being chided about his view of the pastor's visit.

Let's take a look at some of the phrases used…

66 BROD. Pastor put me in mind a ['reminds me of'] Gullyman. (page 37)

It is possible to figure out what this means from the follow-up:

66 BROD. You notice the resemblance?'

66 BROD. […] Him an' him wife. [An interesting construction simply meaning 'the pastor and his wife'.] (page 37)

66 BROD. […] The man too speaky spoky. ['Posh', speaking in Standard English as opposed to **dialect**. The rhyme and sibilance make clear that this is a mocking term, suggesting that someone is being a bit pompous and looking down on others by adopting a more formal register.] (page 37)

66 BROD. [...] she burst out talking in tongues [...] [**Speaking in tongues** is when people utter speech-like sounds or words of an unknown language during a heightened state as part of religious worship. It occurs across various sects of Christianity, but is quite prevalent within some sections of the Black church community both in the Caribbean and Africa.] (page 37)

66 ENID. Quiet nuh, man. ['Keep the noise down, will you?'] (page 37)

As the scene moves to the call from Jamaica, we see Enid continuing to speak patois with her sister:

66 ENID. [...] Cynthia talk to me, nuh. [A request often made when someone is not being clear, as in this case. Cynthia is upset at the bad news she has to convey.] (page 40)

Enid's response to news of Mooma's death is:

66 ENID. Ah lie Cynthia a tell. [This expression not only means 'Cynthia is lying' but also suggests 'I don't understand why she is doing this.' Sometimes there is greater meaning in the words than a basic translation gives.] (page 40)

Scene Four

Setting

66 *Very late that night.* (page 41)

How might the late-night setting affect the way that the actors perform this scene? How does that impact on the relationship between the two characters?

Key points to consider

- This is one of the shortest scenes, but it unpacks so much about Enid's character and many of the themes addressed across the play.

- Viv learns things that she did not know about Enid's life. She is not used to her mum being so open.

- Death often brings on self-reflection and a search for meaning, and Enid attempts to track back over her life to make sense of where she is now.

Key characters and what we learn

Enid

Scene Four reveals to us just how much anxiety and memory of past experiences Enid is suppressing. Again, **imagery** is used, to bring hunger to life as a fierce animal:

66 ENID. Not that little nibbling English lunchtime hunger.
I talking 'bout the sort that roar in your belly day and
night [...] (page 42)

Her **contrast** to 'little nibbling English lunchtime hunger' diminishes the hunger Viv may have experienced herself so that she understands the severity of the poverty Enid experienced as a child.

Structurally, there has been a development in Enid's character since the death of Mooma. From not wanting Viv to know anything about life in Jamaica, she now attempts to contrast Brod's nostalgic stories with a raw truth. We learn about why she felt she had to leave, and Mooma's reaction:

66 ENID. You know, the day I was to leave she never say goodbye
to me? (page 43)

Enid is haunted by this, but she is also trying to convey an understanding of Mooma's motives and how hard life must have been. Perhaps Mooma felt she had failed, and understood why Enid had to leave and try to make a better life.

Enid also talks of her relationship with her husband, their aspirations and shared love:

> 66 ENID. [...] He save every single penny he work to buy that ticket. (page 44)

And yet we know that he is no longer around, and that Enid longs for the life they planned together. Pinnock **mirrors** his saving to bring Enid into that life, in her handing the building society savings account book to Viv. **Symbolically**, Enid transfers that love to Viv with it.

Viv

Viv seeks to console Enid. As Enid opens up and reveals detail about her early life, it is clear that Viv is moved but not quite understanding.

> 66 VIV. You don't live off the land any more. (page 42)

Viv doesn't comprehend the impact this harsh kind of living has had on Enid and how it has shaped her. However, she finally gets to hear what she believes is so often concealed from her ('You never tell us anything' – page 42), discovering how much love her parents had for each other.

Viv makes an essential connection – Enid does not want Viv to have a life of hardship. Viv uses this opportunity to free herself:

> 66 VIV. All right. (*Takes the book.*) All right. (*Slight pause.*) I can't live your life for you. I don't know what you want. (page 45)

She is able to stand up for herself and not live in the shadow of Enid's dreams. This is an important development for Viv, as she knows that she must have hopes and aspirations that are her own.

> *Keywords:*
> **Mirroring** is when writers repeat images of moments, or behaviour, from character to character.
> **Symbolism** is when symbols are used to represent ideas. Here, the saved money Enid gives represents love.

Task

Think about the staging of this scene, and write some notes to help you visualise how you might present it if you were the director. Make a list of **props** and how you would position Viv and Enid on stage.

Model paragraph

> ### *What do we learn about Mooma and her relationship with Enid in this scene?*
>
> While Enid is clearly very hurt by Mooma's rejection when she left Jamaica, many of her memories in Scene Four show that Mooma actually loved her. For example, intimacy is demonstrated by Mooma taking Enid 'on a long walk' to 'secret places'. However, Enid did not understand this unexplained demonstration of love, as we learn when she says 'I don't know why' (page 43). It is clear that Mooma was better at showing her love with actions than with words. Enid's nostalgic remark: 'I have a taste for a big cup a Mooma chocolate tea' (page 43) demonstrates how Pinnock is able to inject flavours of the Caribbean into these reminiscences, appealing to the audience's senses, as well as Viv's, to create a vivid **image**.

Writing task – you try it!

How does Viv's relationship with Enid compare with Enid's relationship with Mooma?

Write about:

- Viv and Enid, and Viv's need to please her mum.
- Lack of communication and understanding in both sets of relationships.
- How love is conveyed.
- Make reference to other parts of the play before Scene Four.

Context and emerging themes

Read over the section in the Context chapter from page 14 about life in Jamaica and reasons why people came to the UK. Pinnock gives us an insight into the real-life experiences of 'leave taking' through her characters: the pressure of building a better life here as well as supporting those back home.

Language

This scene is full of memories, regret, bitterness and reflection. Whilst Pinnock has Viv interjecting occasionally, Enid speaks at length, often without responding to Viv's interjections, so that at times it feels as though her **monologue** of memories and **rhetorical questions** is just spoken aloud to herself.

> **Understanding patois**
>
> red up she face = put on blusher
>
> hard dough bread = a Caribbean bread
>
> breadfruit = a starchy vegetable from the jackfruit family, native to the Caribbean and other tropical areas
>
> callaloo = a green leafy vegetable
>
> tek = take
>
> cutlass = machete
>
> breed me up = make me pregnant

Scene Five

Setting

66 *A few weeks later. MAI's room. Midday. MAI takes cards from a pile on the table and places them face up. She takes up a saucer on which is a heap of salt. She sprinkles salt around the room.*

At the beginning of this scene, salt is shown to hold great significance. Research how and why salt is associated with value and superstition, both in Caribbean and UK culture.

Key points to consider

- Del is intrigued by Mai and whilst the generational and cultural barrier has blocked her relationship with Enid, Del is able to establish an easier relationship with Mai.

- The theme of families is layered into the scene as we consider the composition and breakdown of Mai's family, and the conflict in Del's family, as well as Del's impending family, to be established with her unborn child.

- Viv comes to understand that she is more than just her academic success.

- Both girls are moving into adulthood and womanhood and this scene explores how they anticipate and approach the challenges.

Key characters and what we learn

Del

Del clearly remembers Mai's offer in Scene One, and has turned to her for shelter. Pinnock conveys the importance of community here but also a sense that Del is attracted to knowing more about her culture through the obeah tradition.

Del is restless, and whilst she is grateful for Mai's assistance she is sensitive to being told what to do:

66 DEL. I need a sermon I'll go to church. (page 48)

However, she soon realises that there are consequences to her actions when Mai has a 'dizzy spell'. We have seen much of Del's angry and provocative side, but in this scene Del becomes more three-dimensional and displays compassion and affection for Mai.

She sees an opportunity to make amends and that Mai is showing concern rather than wanting to control her. This is an important shift for Del as it paves the way to understanding and finding common ground with Enid later.

We also see a maturity emerging in Del in the way she deals with Viv abandoning her exams:

> DEL. So, you turn bad gyal now? Am I supposed to be impressed? I am not impressed, Viv. (page 53)

It is interesting that she adopts **patois** here with the word 'gyal', invoking the older generation in order to bring Viv to her senses. As Mai deduces from her reading of Del's palm, Del values education, and it is clear that her conflicts with Enid are different from the pressures Viv feels:

> DEL.[...] (*Throwing* VIV's *bag after her.*) And don't come back unless it's to show me a fucking certificate. (page 54)

It would have been easy for Del to assist Viv in her self-sabotage, but Del's growing maturity, and perhaps the aspirations she has for her own child, see her stand firm against Viv's rebellion.

Viv

This scene sees Viv at a crossroads between being a child/teenager and becoming an adult/woman. She feels confined and wants to step away from family conflicts and being perceived as the 'good' one.

> VIV. I always do what everyone else wants me to. From now on I'm gonna do what I want. (page 53)

Viv wants to be seen differently, and it is as if she is trying out Del's rebellious tactics. In allowing Del to compel her to go and complete her exams, Viv is moving towards an understanding of herself and how she can achieve while also remaining true to herself.

Mai

Mai realises that Del is sceptical of her powers and decides to address Del's goading by reading her palm:

> 66 MAI. [...] The teachers say you slow, so you give up [...] but just recently you have had a change of heart. (page 47)

She cuts right to the heart of Del's issues and wins Del's grudging respect. It might be that she is already seeing Del's potential. We also see Mai's maternal instincts in the way that she is protective of Del, but at the same time, Mai is not prepared to engage with Del in an antagonistic way or one that mirrors Del's relationship with Enid:

> 66 MAI. Don't speak to me like that. You think I'm your mother? (page 48)

Mai asserts how she wants to be treated, drawing boundaries whilst ensuring that an open line for communication remains. She enjoys having Del around but also recognises that she must offer guidance to Del as an elder.

Model paragraph

> ### How does Pinnock portray Del and Viv's dissatisfaction with education in this scene?

Keyword: A **simile** is a form of imagery where something is described as resembling something else. It is usually signalled with the word 'like' or 'as'.

Del and Viv have different experiences of education: Viv has been very successful and is seen as intelligent, whereas Del has dropped out of school. In this scene Pinnock reveals through Mai that there is a reason why Del hated school and why teachers thought she wasn't bright, as Mai uses the **simile** 'like black ants' (page 47) to create the image of words escaping and confusing Del. This helps to explain Del's attitude to school and work, and that she may have dyslexia. It could be that she is as intelligent as Viv but did not receive any support from school, causing her to lose motivation.

Writing task – you try it!

What do we learn about Del and her relationship with Enid by observing her relationship with Mai?

Write about:

- Her initial attitude to Mai as the scene opens.

- How it changes.

- Mai's comments on Del's behaviour.

- What Del wants from both of these relationships.

- What she gets from Mai but not from Enid.

Context and emerging themes

This scene focuses on the themes of family and the reconfiguring of families, as Mai and Del bond. It also explores education and how Black children were treated within the education system. Teenage pregnancy also emerges as a theme, as Viv laments Del's surroundings, and explores what her own role will be as an aunt. Del asserts her intention not to continue her relationship with Roy in spite of the stigma associated with teenage pregnancy and single-parenting.

Themes: For more on family, turn to page 126.

Context: To read more about the context of Black children in the British education system, turn to page 28. To read more about attitudes towards teenage pregnancy, turn to page 27.

Language

Whilst the Caribbean **dialect** is chiefly depicted through Mai in this scene, Del also falls into using it by mimicking her:

❝ DEL. [...] If me wrong say me wrong. (page 49)

This provides a moving, yet humorous moment. Most Caribbean children were discouraged from speaking patois as their parents wanted them to be 'English', but they would still use patois in jest to humour adults, to confirm understanding, show anger, or characterise a person in an anecdote.

> *Keywords:*
> **Expletives** are swear words.
> **Colloquialisms** are informal terms used within particular communities.

Between Del and Viv, Del switches to patois to show her anger at Viv's decision, however the bulk of their exchange is in their London **dialect** and it is peppered with **expletives** and **colloquialisms** (like 'lingo'). Viv's language moves between Standard English, London **dialect**, and the imaginative flowery language of the literature she loves. Del is far more direct. There are echoes of the patterns of storytelling from their Caribbean influence coming through and this hints at the way that Black culture and **dialect** has influenced the way many people in London converse, as groups mix, blend and communicate.

Scene Six

Setting

Mai is 'concentrating' over Enid's palm-reading as the scene opens with a comedic moment, which is contrasted with how the rest of the scene unfolds. We are reminded of Scene One, when Mai was keen to get money and be done with the reading, as she lazily points to information she is likely to know through Del and Viv: 'You going on a long journey', follows up with some very basic advice: 'So you better look out you passport', and ends with, 'that will be fifteen pounds.' (page 54). The *'Beat.'* pauses that Pinnock inserts in this speech are a theatrical device which heighten the comedy. It is a light moment for the audience, as both women reveal very raw emotions after this.

Key points to consider

- The theme of identity is expressed through Mai and Enid as they discuss their sense of loss and failure in coming to the UK.

- Parenting is also a theme at the heart of this scene.

- Guilt is explored through Enid's reflection on Mooma's passing, as well as Mai concealing the truth about Del's whereabouts.

- Historical references to slavery and the impact of migration are expressed in Mai's thoughts to Del at the end of the scene.

Key characters and what we learn

Mai

This scene is powerful as it depicts two Black women showing what they 'know about a black woman soul' (page 56) and attempting to heal and comfort each other. Mai bonds and empathises with Enid, reflecting on and having a new perspective on the problems that led to her own son leaving. She reveals the real trauma of leaving your home when she says, 'It mash up you life.' (page 56), and she remarks upon the fact that the children of the Windrush generation are struggling:

> MAI. [...] When I see them children on the TV, so angry and betrayed... Whuh! (page 56)

She is trying to let Enid know that she now understands and sees how hard it is for them.

Mai may come across as disingenuous, because as soon as Enid departs she grumbles:

> MAI. [...] expect me to reach into their souls and stick the broken pieces back together. (page 57)

However this does not negate the moving conversation they have shared.

Enid

We feel a great deal of sympathy and empathy for Enid in this scene. She is grieving, and feeling guilty and responsible for her mother's death:

> ENID. If I did send that money home she wouldna die. (page 56)

She is also missing Del, and worries about whether she has failed her children and herself in coming to the UK. We see Enid breaking down under the strain of all this, and the moment of release is extremely dramatic, with one of the most detailed actor **stage directions** in the play:

> *Standing,* ENID *stares straight ahead, then her face contorts and her mouth opens in a soundless scream. Then the sound comes – a howl of pain* [...] ENID *sobs quietly then pulls herself together.* (page 56)

Here we see that Enid always feels a need to be strong, but she cannot help but question and mock her own innocent aspirations in coming to the UK in the first place:

> ENID. Is this I come here for? Look at me. (*Smiles, bitter.*) Miss English. (page 56)

Pinnock's stage direction for Enid: 'Smiles, bitter' reinforces her **tone**. Enid feels that her decisions and lofty dreams are unravelling.

Tasks

1. Reread the Context chapter from page 24 and make notes about some of the issues facing children and young people of the Windrush generation and how they relate to this scene.

2. Mai's son is older than Del and Viv but seems to have struggled with identity and belonging in the same way. Write or improvise a scene that explores what they would say to each other if they met.

3. Act the scene out and take feedback from your classmates.

Model paragraph

> **How do Mai's feelings about her son mirror Enid's about Del in this scene?**

Mai and Enid respond to their conflict with their children in similar ways. Both women feel they have made sacrifices in moving to Britain in order to give their children better opportunities. However, both children feel **ostracised** by the society they have grown up in, and Mai and Enid have come to realise this. In Scene Six, Enid says 'Over here the children can't live like normal people' (page 55). Enid's idea of 'normal' in this context is British people, and she sees that Del and Viv's background prevents them ultimately from fitting in. Meanwhile, as Mai looks back on her son, she remembers 'He used to tell me how he never feel even a little bit British' (page 57), the phrase 'even a little bit' emphasising the extent of her son's disaffection. Both Mai and Enid take responsibility in this scene for their feeling that they have let their children down. Mai says 'I was hard on my boy. I didn't hate him. I was trying to save him' (page 57), while Enid says 'Our children are right to blame us' (page 55). This understanding that the children's heritage and skin colour prevents them from truly feeling they belong is a step towards the reconciliation Pinnock depicts at the end of the play.

Writing task – you try it!

'DEL. How can you love yourself when you're always bottom of the pile?' (page 58)

What do we learn about the impact of life in Britain for the characters in Scene Six?

Write about:

- Racism.

- Generational divide.

> *Themes:* You can read more about these themes from page 119.

Context and emerging themes

This scene focuses sharply on the negative impact coming to Britain has had on both generations. It also looks at how parents struggled to see the issues that their children experienced, and that the opportunities did not always outweigh the pitfalls of racism and the need for a sense of identity and belonging.

> *Keyword:* **Dramatic irony** is when information known to the reader or audience is not known to the character(s) in a scene.

Language

One of the key literary devices employed in this scene is **dramatic irony**, as we the audience know that Del is staying at Mai's, but of course Enid is unaware of this. This creates **tension**, and anticipation that the scene could descend into **conflict**. We also see how this scenario impacts Mai, through her responses and in her expressions of guilt to Del.

Scene Seven

Setting

❝ MAI's *living room. Very early the next morning.* BROD *lies stretched out on the table.* DEL *is looking down at him quizzically. She puts her hand to his face, checks his breathing, lifts his hand and lets it flop back. She puts her ear to his chest.* MAI *stands beside her, carrying a mug of water.*
(page 58)

> *Keyword:* A **metaphor** is a form of imagery where a thing is described indirectly by referring to something it resembles, without using 'like'.

In the other scenes at Mai's bedsit much of the action takes place around the table, so it is **symbolic** that in this scene Broderick is actually *on* the table, as if his life is **metaphorically** 'on the table' as the topic of discussion. Pinnock returns to her regular structural device of opening a scene with a comic moment. The audience, Del and Mai, all wonder at first whether Brod is dead, but tension is released when Mai asks 'Him dead?' and Del responds 'Not yet', after which, instead of getting Brod to drink the water as we might expect, Mai throws it over his face.

Key points to consider

- Broderick as a vehicle for presenting male voices in the play.
- Racism and its dehumanising impact.
- Del's reaction to Brod and her relationship with him.
- Enid's state of mind and her mental health.
- Brod's relationship with Enid.
- What Mai sees in Del at the end of the scene.

Key characters and what we learn

Broderick

It is clear that Broderick has a drinking problem and is possibly an alcoholic. We see that there is an underlying unhappiness in Broderick, and that events he relates have taken their toll.

Brod's role as a father figure and teacher unravels in this scene as he turns to Del for help and solace, telling Mai:

> 66 BROD. I wanted to speak to my young friend. There was something I had was to tell her. (page 60)

We don't find out exactly what Broderick wanted to tell Del when he was drunk, but we get a strong impression that he needs to express some of the reasons for his failings, and those of Del's father. Brod's story about Del's father mirrors his story in Scene Two about Gullyman. Like Gullyman, Brod explores how Enid's husband's experience of racism affected his mind:

> 66 BROD. Now, he was a madman. I never see a man eyes look so empty. (page 60)

Pinnock explores the way racism has impacted on their sense of pride and worth as men, and Brod implies that challenges to Enid's husband's very humanity at work (with racist abusers calling him an animal: "'Show us yer tail, yer black monkey'" – page 62) made him want to assert his masculinity at home: "'You give big man food with no salting?'" (page 62).

However, Pinnock also points to ideas about taking personal responsibility:

> BROD. [...] I'm not saying he wouldna do the same thing if he was back home, what I saying is that coming here speeden things up because no one care what he want to do to a black woman. (page 62)

Brod's partial excusing of Enid's husband's behaviour contrasts with the women in the play who have experienced similar indignities but did not abandon their families and responsibilities. Pinnock perhaps is showing that masculinity under threat is fragile and can break men down, whereas for many women it is different. The impact of racism may challenge their femininity but also strengthens their innate role as mothers to protect their children and find a way through. Broderick and the other men seem to just give up, and in some way feel justified in their actions:

> BROD. I didn't run away. Yes, I went wild for a time [...] I made mistakes but that didn't give her the right to say I couldn't see my kids [...] (page 62)

Pinnock suggests that women are held to a higher standard in society, and Broderick reinforces this in his references to Nanny of the Maroons.

Del

Del reveals another source of her frustration in this scene by expressing her anger towards men. This deepens our understanding of her and her motives. Men have been absent in her life and have let her down, and so her determination to raise her child on her own is driven by this. Even though she can talk to Broderick, she does not view him any differently, and she reverses his challenge about her life:

“ DEL. [...] And what about you, Brod? Do you see your wife and kids? (page 62)

This is a sarcastic **rhetorical question** as Del clearly knows that he is estranged from his family. Through Del we see that all the characters are suppressing how they really feel, and seem unable to deal with issues negatively impacting their lives. The **stage directions** show Del attempting to process all that Brod has said:

“ DEL *walks up and down the room.* [...] DEL *kicks a wall in frustration.* (page 63)

Del is beginning to see how difficult things have been for Enid. Through Mai and now Brod she is presented with the way in which these experiences may well be central to the friction between them.

Mai

Mai's relationship with the family is sorely tested in this scene and we see her frustration:

“ MAI. Minute I set eye 'pon that Enid Matthews I know say the woman was trouble. I did read it in she palm. (page 60)

Mai feels entangled in the problems of the family and her stress causes her to **exaggerate** her actual feelings about Enid. It is interesting and **ironic** that by the end of the scene she arrives at the real purpose for meeting Enid:

> Keyword: **Irony** is when something said or a moment in the plot is deliberately the opposite of what is expected.

“ MAI. And now I see it plain plain. (page 64)

Mai begins to see Del's true calling, and we circle back to Scene One where she offered Del the opportunity to talk. Mai ponders over retiring in this scene, so her realisation about Del seems a fitting **plot device** and offers cultural continuity.

> Keyword: A **plot device** is a technique designed to move the narrative forward.

Task

Even though Enid isn't in this scene, we learn some significant things about her life and state of mind. Make a list of what we find out about Enid as the scene unfolds.

Model paragraph

> **How does Pinnock explore ideas about gender roles in this scene?**

While the majority of *Leave Taking* is centred on female experience, in Scene Seven, Pinnock explores the male perspective in greater depth through Brod. In doing so, she shows a distinction between the resilience of her female characters and that of her male characters against adversity. Brod explains that he drinks because 'It help me forget' (page 61). It is clear from the word 'forget' that there are parts of Brod's past he is trying to erase with alcohol. This is in stark **contrast** to Enid, who 'Say she carry too many people for too long' (page 59). Where Enid has supported others through difficulty, Brod has tried to shut out the world. It is also clear that Brod expects this supportive behaviour from Enid. He expresses concern that she has not been herself since Del's departure, and his evidence is that 'She don't clean, she don't cook' – both are aspects of traditional female gender roles. Meanwhile, Del, disillusioned with the lack of responsibility she sees in Brod and other men like him, asks 'What makes you men allergic to the sound of a baby crying?' (page 62). Her **metaphorical** use of 'allergic' highlights how strongly she feels men avoid the responsibility of fatherhood. Although Brod is a sympathetic character, and provides much of the humour in the play, Pinnock uses him, and his story about Del's father, to explore ideas about poor male role models.

Writing task – you try it!

Comment on the role of men as explored in Scene Seven.

Write about:

- Family structures and absent fathers.
- Racism.
- Domestic violence.
- Masculinity.

Context and emerging themes

Brod speaks of racism and how it can amplify negative aspects of one's personality. The changing role of men and women generally is also an important factor, as we see the women in the play forging forward in spite of the absence of partners and husbands.

Language

This scene continues to build on the devices and conventions used throughout the play. Through Broderick, Pinnock employs the technique of the **monologue** or **soliloquy** by combining it with the **oral tradition** of **storytelling** popular in Caribbean cultures.

> *Keyword:* A **soliloquy** is when a character speaks their thoughts aloud, either alone on stage or without any other characters who are onstage hearing or responding.

We see how this device is used to relate stories both of humour and fond memories, and more sombre commentaries on the harsh realities of life in Jamaica and the UK. Pinnock uses it to comment on Broderick's life, the role of racism and the role of men.

Like the other stories, Broderick's tale in this scene is compact and yet complete, carefully choosing the moments to highlight in order to move the storytelling to its conclusion.

❝ BROD. [...] If they won't treat him like a human being outside, him make sure she treat him like a king in him own house [...] (page 62)

Sentences like this, with its internal balance of comparisons between 'human being' and 'king', powerfully sum up the impact of racism and feeling powerless, being overpowered, and abusing power.

Pinnock also uses other literary devices, including **hyperbole**, to show how the characters have a heightened sense of what they are experiencing, such as Broderick pretending to be homeless ('she kick me out into the street with nowhere to go' – page 59), and Mai exaggerating the repercussions of meeting Enid.

A **tone** of sarcasm is used to convey Del's feelings about Broderick's behaviour, as she **repeats**:

> 66 DEL. Poor Uncle Brod. (pages 60–61)

She does not mean this, and is in fact running out of patience with him. Pinnock also uses a common speech pattern in patois where words are repeated for emphasis, such as when Mai starts to see Del's gift:

> 66 MAI. And now I see it plain plain. (page 64)

'Plain' means that she can see things clearly, but the **repetition** delivers greater impact. This pattern is used across the various Caribbean islands (mirroring West African languages) and is an effective way of expressing a sense of urgency or understanding behind what is being said.

Humour is also used to contrast with heavier aspects of this scene, such as when Mai expresses her disapproval of Brod:

> 66 MAI. You know this old tramp? (page 59)

This is humorous as we know Broderick, but to Mai he is simply cluttering her space, and she isn't concerned that he can hear what she is saying. Brod is often the main source of comic relief and in this scene he uses humour to deflect, and to offer yet more takes on why he drinks:

Keyword: **Repetition** is a literary technique often used by writers for emphasis.

❝ BROD. Poor Broderick James. A man condemn to roam the earth from public house to public house in search of that elusive perfect beer. (page 60)

Irony and humour are combined here, because as the scene unfolds, we discover more about his desire to lose himself to escape life's realities. In the final scene, we are left wondering whether Broderick is out there on his quest or whether he and Enid have reconciled.

Scene Eight

Setting

The description of Mai's room in the opening **stage directions** can be **contrasted** with Scene One. It is clear that Del's presence is having some positive impact.

Key points to consider

- Del and Mai's relationship has deepened.

- Del has matured and found an interest and career path that she is happy with. She is still young and teases Mai playfully, but recognises and responds appropriately when Mai expects her to.

- Whilst Viv is not included in this scene, we discover that she has found the courage to pursue her interests and heritage.

- The play ends with two powerful stories of mothers and daughters, and the way love is expressed, detected and absent. Del and Enid find peace and respect for each other and are reconciled.

Key characters and what we learn

Mai

In this scene we discover that Mai is very ill, possibly dying, but in spite of this, the scene's **tone** is one of optimism. Mai is hopeful and rejuvenated by having Del as her apprentice and heir:

> MAI. I don't have a daughter to pass them on to. And my son... well, he isn't interested. (page 69)

It makes her happy to think that the tradition of obeah will not die out with her, and whilst Del continues to feign reluctance, Mai instinctively knows that Del is the right person to continue 'the old ways':

> MAI. What you doing here if you not keeping them alive? (page 66)

Where Mai may have failed in her relationship with her son, she is keen to make amends by succeeding with Del. Mai is able to bring out the best of Del's qualities, and help her to channel her anger and discontent. She gently and playfully reminds Del of her tough exterior:

> MAI. You nervous? What happen to big tough Del? You will be all right. (page 70)

Mai has been able to see Del's potential from the beginning, and demonstrates how parenting and mentoring are universally important for young people. Mai wants Del to feel trusted and confident in her abilities, but she is also steering her towards finding the maturity to reconcile with Enid.

Del

The contrast in Del's character is perhaps the most stark. Del's relationship with Mai has enabled her to find validation and self-worth. She has resisted reconciling with Enid up to now, but Mai's intervention is at a point when Del is happier within herself and can see a future.

The relationship she has established with Mai is what she wants from Enid – Del feels that it's all right to be herself around Mai and it is apparent that she has learned to recognise her own shortcomings and not argue with Mai. She is able to identify Mai's admonishments as guidance and simply replies, 'All right, Mai.'

Del is still confused and wants her mother's approval but recognises in her final story that she received love and loved her mother as a child:

> 66 DEL. [...] It was like there was heat and light coming off you. [...] Then you'd go and we'd have kisses on our cheeks. We could still smell you, warm in the room. (pages 71–72)

But the conflict with the way their relationship played out has the thought: 'Why don't you like me?' running alongside a memory of love. This is echoed in Enid's story, but the scene ends in hope, and we see Del break the cycle of concealed love, restraint and hurt:

> 66 DEL *has a struggle with herself. Then she makes a decision. She joins* ENID *at the table and takes her mother's hand into both her own and smooths the palm with her thumbs.* (page 72)

This is a powerful image, and through it Pinnock shows that the younger generation can lead the way in breaking the cycle and trying to understand what sacrifices their parents have made for good and ill.

Enid

Enid comes to an understanding in this scene. She realises that she cannot live her life through the girls. She accepts Viv's choices, even though she doesn't quite understand them:

❝ ENID. Black Studies. You ever hear of such a thing? (page 71)

However, in many ways, her final story demonstrates that she does understand. It cannot escape Del that Enid's words echo her own distress about how she was treated at work, in Scene Two:

❝ ENID. Nobody see you, nobody hear you. [...] People walk through you like you not there [...] (page 72)

Enid tries here to explain to Del that it was almost an impossible task to face the alienation and hostility and to guide her children through it:

❝ ENID. [...] How you going teach you children that they don't exist? (page 72)

Enid expresses a feeling of helplessness, and Del is invited to realise how difficult it was for Enid, and that alongside denial, her attempt to ensure that the girls conformed and did well in their education was the only solution she had.

Enid's thoughts on her own relationship with her mother is a further attempt to illustrate to Del how society constrains the way in which you are able to love your children.

❝ ENID. [...] Right up to the end she never say a word to me. (page 72)

Enid's story shows her wanting to break that cycle with Del and Viv.

Enid expresses a need to be truly loved, and realises that her hard exterior alienates her children. She realises that she is able to give and receive love, 'like Mooma never could'.

> ✏ **Playwright insight:**
>
> 'When I reflect on that last speech. I always think you can't write a speech like that unless you have experienced something like it. I think that as a twenty-three-year-old, I understood how the world sees a Black woman. So it's not really just about Mooma. Mooma is there to represent history, almost. There's a sort of historical way in which Black women have been looked down on and discriminated against. When Enid says "how do you teach your children that you know that this is going to happen to them?", my mum must have asked that question. It is bigger than just the domestic. It isn't just about one woman saying this to another. It's a bigger thing about the way in which Black women are perceived.'

Task

Think of two or three questions you would ask each of the characters about how they feel about their lives at the end of Scene Eight, and write their responses. You could work with a partner or in threes, and take it turns to ask the questions and answer in character. Challenge each other to use evidence from the whole play in your responses.

Model paragraph

> **How does Pinnock create a feeling of hopefulness in the final scene?**

In the final scene, Pinnock offers resolution to some of the difficulties characters have faced in the play, as well as depicting a greater understanding between them, and a reconciliation leading to hope for the future. Del's disaffection and lack of qualifications has held her back in the past, so it is significant that in Scene Eight, Mai tells her 'You got to take your exams' (page 66). Although these 'exams' are informal, they represent Del's new place within her community as Mai's successor, and offer hope for both Del and the wider Caribbean culture in London after the predicted death of Mai. Qualifications also feature in the resolution of Viv's inner conflict, as we learn that she is 'packing up to go to university' to study 'Black Studies' (page 71). This means that she will further her own interest in her heritage while fulfilling Enid's ambition for her. Understanding is key to the reconciliation between Enid and Del. In their final exchange, Enid says, 'You say I don't see how them treat you out there. I see it. I see it and it makes me want to tear the place down.' (page 72) Her **repetition** of 'I see it' emphasises her recognition of Del's struggle, while the violence in the phrase 'tear the place down' mirrors the anger Del expressed about the injustice of their treatment in Scene Two. Pinnock depicts a beginning to the resolution of conflict between Del and Enid, and hope for the future now that Enid sees things from Del's point of view.

Writing task – you try it!

What do we learn about the importance of motherhood in the final scene?

Think about:

- Del's relationship with Mai.

- Mai acting as a mother for all the characters.

- Enid's relationship with her daughters and with Mooma.

- The importance of guidance, approval and love.

- Make reference to other parts of the play, too.

Context and final themes

Pinnock explores the struggles of both generations, and whilst Broderick talks of having his Jamaican passport at hand, the final scene demonstrates how acknowledging their roots, traditions and struggles leads to there being a place and future for all of them in the UK. The characters begin to understand each other, learn from their experiences, and find new ways to bond, support and respect each other.

Language

Pinnock ends with the powerful **storytelling** device as Del and Enid relate their tales to each other. Enid's story moves from a **monologue** to a direct plea to Del:

66 ENID. [...] But now is up to you. I been fighting too long, Del. (page 72)

This **mirrors** Del's story where she vividly recalls the childhood comfort her mother gave her, and then ends with a plea in the question:

66 DEL. Why don't you like me? (page 72)

Pinnock enables her characters to be more direct and honest with their feelings in this scene. Where elsewhere the characters' true feelings can be gleaned through **subtext,** here their language conveys exactly how the characters have been feeling throughout the play, so that in Scene Eight they gain answers and understanding.

All photos are of the 2018 revival of *Leave Taking* at the Bush Theatre, London, directed by Madani Younis, and show the following scenes in the play (page numbers refer to the Nick Hern Books edition of the text):

- *Photo 1*: **Scene Two (*page 26*)**, Sarah Niles as Enid and Wil Johnson as Brod
- *Photo 2*: **Scene Two (*page 31*)**, Sarah Niles as Enid
- *Photo 3*: **Scene Three (*page 38*)**, Wil Johnson as Brod and Sarah Niles as Enid
- *Photo 4*: **Scene Four (*page 41*)**, Sarah Niles as Enid and Nicholle Cherrie as Viv
- *Photo 5*: **Scene Five (*page 53*)**, Nicholle Cherrie as Viv
- *Photo 6*: **Scene Eight (*page 68*)**, Seraphina Beh as Del and Adjoa Andoh as Mai

All photos by Helen Murray/ArenaPAL (www.arenapal.com)

Characters

Enid

How does Pinnock present the character of Enid?

Characteristics:
- Proud
- God-fearing
- Purposeful
- Suspicious/distrusting
- Hard-working
- Secretive
- Repressed/suppressed

What does Enid represent?
- A matriarch
- A migrant
- The **Windrush generation**

Enid is a Jamaican migrant of the Windrush generation

Enid is in her forties and arrived in England before her daughters were born, to seek more opportunities. She is the product of colonial heritage. Her upbringing would have taught her to regard England as the '**Mother Country**'. She is aware of the effect of colonialism on her home country – her sister's children do not have the same privileges hers have been afforded in England; her sister's children do not get to go to university due to poverty and limited opportunities. Enid has

assimilated to some degree, and has made England her home, gaining citizenship. Her objective is to give her children better opportunities than she had:

66 ENID. You come here, you try to fit in. Stick to the rules. England been good to me. I proud a my English girls. (Scene Two, page 29)

She has high expectations of her children and is proud of her youngest daughter's decision to go to university. When Del loses her job, Enid demands she gets another, perhaps for fear of bringing shame on the family. Enid's generation was worried about being seen as 'lazy' – a stereotype attached to Caribbean migrants when they first arrived.

Enid is a single mother

Enid was 'sent for' by her husband who saved his salary for a year to afford her ticket. As the result of a tumultuous relationship, she has been left to raise two children on her own:

66 ENID. Me husban' long gone, yes. But I don't want him back. I bring up those two girls on me own. (Scene One, page 17)

Divorce, particularly in the Black community, was taboo and frowned upon due to strong Christian beliefs in the sacrament of marriage and biblical teachings that encourage family values.

We get the impression that the burden of motherhood has been heavy:

66 ENID. Our children are right to blame us. If we can't give them a good life we shouldn't have them. (Scene Six, page 55)

Enid blames herself for the misfortunes of Del's position and worries that her mothering hasn't been enough. She alludes to the struggle of parenting alone when she says:

66 ENID. I have to be man and woman, shout so them hear me and when I hear meself I think, why that woman shouting so? (Scene Six, page 55)

The burden of being both mother and father is something she finds hard to manage, and she clearly feels hopeless, and perhaps that her efforts are failing.

Enid is a hard-working woman who has had to struggle to make ends meet. She is a product of the societal barriers suffered by most Black single mothers, and indeed single women, to things such as renting property, home ownership, and anything other than menial labour. Image is important to Enid, and she doesn't want her children to carry the shame of not having a father. She dresses them in fine clothes and makes sacrifices to compensate for the absence of their father:

66 ENID. [...] People laugh at me, but they never laugh at you. (Scene Three, page 34)

We learn from Brod in Scene Two that Enid didn't achieve her dream of becoming a postmistress as she never passed the exam. Despite all this, Enid does draw upon her inner strength in navigating her way through the difficulties of raising two children alone.

Enid had a difficult childhood in Jamaica

Enid grew up in a poor agricultural setting, often going without basic necessities:

66 ENID. [...] The land fail you, you might as well be dead. (Scene Four, page 42)

Evidently agricultural labour was hard and often left them hungry. Enid expresses how the circumstances of her upbringing made her feel both 'shy' and a sense of 'shame', when she met her uncle's American wife (Scene Four, page 42). It is clear that these emotions travelled with her to the UK and into adulthood. She also has a sense of duty and obligation to send money back home, having managed to escape to England where the currency is stronger and she is able to provide a financial cushion for her family in Jamaica.

Enid is suspicious and distrustful

At the start of the play, Enid is suspicious of her sister's request that she send money back home to take care of her mother's medical needs:

66 ENID. [...] A month ago me sister send me this letter say me mother sick, need money for doctor. The woman so lie. I don't know whether to believe her or not. (Scene One, page 18)

Even though she is distrustful of her sister, Enid evidently feels a sense of obligation to support her family in Jamaica.

There is a cultural barrier between Enid and her daughter Del

Enid questions Del's way of life when conversing with Mai:

66 ENID. She getting outta hand. She don't come home after work. (Scene One, page 20)

> Keyword:
> **Anglophone** –
> English speaking.

Enid is disconnected from the younger generation's values and culture. Whilst she is an **anglophone** woman, her core cultural and value systems are rooted in her Caribbean upbringing, and there is a communication barrier between Enid and her children; Viv says 'you lot never tell me anything' (page 32), suggesting that Enid may have put up a wall between them for various reasons. One can assume that the trauma she has suffered as a Caribbean migrant is too painful to relive, and perhaps her coping mechanism is to bury and suppress these experiences in order to survive and to protect her daughters from her humiliation.

Enid also feels rejected by her mother:

66 ENID. [...] Mooma never like me. [...] I was too black, me hair too dry, everything that make you invisible in the world. (Scene Eight, page 72)

> Keyword:
> **Colourism** refers to
> the idea that lighter
> skin is more
> desirable because
> of its closer
> proximity to
> European ideals of
> beauty.

Enid felt her mother's rejection had to do with **colourism** and her being of a darker skin tone. However, the key moment of rejection when Enid left for England may have been because Mooma felt betrayed by Enid going so far away, or felt sad and didn't want to show it.

Enid is a follower of two conflicting forms of spirituality

Enid is a **paradox** – anchored to Christian values and yet seeking answers through Mai the obeah woman. Church is an integral part of her identity and shapes her worldview. She reveres the church and makes a fuss when the pastor comes to visit their home, trying to ensure that everything is perfect. His approval is clearly important to her. In a similar way, Enid thinks highly of Mai and insists on her daughters being respectful in Mai's home.

> *Keyword:* A **paradox** is something that seems to have contradictory qualities.

Enid's character development

More than any other character, Pinnock's development of Enid's character becomes a key part of the play's form and structure. The narrative arc is tied to Enid's emotional journey, as she develops from a place of defiance and denial, and a lack of understanding with her daughters, to a greater openness and mutual understanding.

Turn to page 139 for more detail about the play's structure, and to page 141 to read about the key turning point for Enid in the play.

Del

How does Pinnock present the character of Del?

Characteristics:

- Assertive
- Confident
- Argumentative
- Spiritual

What does Del represent?

- The second-generation Black British experience

Del is a second-generation Black British teenager

Del is coming of age. She is the eldest daughter, at eighteen, and clashes with Enid due to the cultural differences between the two generations. Born and brought up in London, Del has a completely different worldview to Enid. She rejects traditional Caribbean practices of spirituality, and the obeah woman. When the audience first meets Del, she appears to be judgemental and rude:

> ❝ DEL. [...] (*Stands and looks around the room.*) What a mess. I bet there's rats. (Scene One, page 16)

Del represents how second-generation Black British-born people had to carve their way through the social and political unrest caused by increasing racial harassment and the biased use of the **sus law**. Tensions between the police and Black communities characterise the context in which Del is becoming a woman. Like her mother's generation, Del faces discrimination in the workplace because of her race: 'He talks to me as if I can't speak English' (page 33). However, unlike her mother, she is vocal about her mistreatment:

Context: Turn to page 25 for more detail about the sus law.

> ❝ DEL. [...] You don't see the police vans hunting us down, or the managers who treat us like we're the lowest of the low. You're too busy bowing and scraping to your beloved England. (Scene Two, page 34)

Del recognises the hardship and oppression that her mother's generation has endured, but instead forms part of a new generation insisting on change and equality.

Del struggles to accept obeah practices

Del speculates that the obeah woman is only concerned with profiting from her mother. Initially, she dismisses the power of obeah, and her ideas align with European notions associating obeah practices with sorcery and wizardry. She suggests that obeah is foolish: 'Duppies and evil spirits. Give us a break' (page 24), and she clearly wants no part of it.

But even though Del is British-born, she is still deeply influenced by her Caribbean heritage. Whilst she appears to reject the obeah practices at the start of the play, she eventually succumbs to Mai's way of life when she takes up residency with her. In some ways Del's character is a vehicle for maintaining Caribbean traditions and legacy. It is through obeah practices that Del can reconnect with her lost history and in some ways retrieve an aspect of her African identity.

As the play progresses, Del becomes more curious and inquisitive about Mai's practices. In Scene Five she quizzes Mai about her deceased husband: 'Do you ever talk to him... his spirit?', and her son, asking: 'Can't you use the obeah to find him?' (page 46). Clearly Del is curious about the power of obeah practices and yearns for knowledge to connect with her own spirituality.

Del has a difficult relationship with Enid

Enid's conflict with Del could also be reflective of how similar Del is to her mother. Viv points out that they are 'Both as bad as each other' (page 17). Enid attempts to understand Del through Mai and her reading. She is concerned that Del spends nights out: 'She getting outta hand. She don't come home after work.' (page 20) Del, like many young second-generation Caribbean migrants of the seventies and eighties, is influenced by the emerging sound systems and blues parties in London; she is enthralled by this culture and like many young people wants to explore and have fun. Less influenced by strict religious ideologies, she breaks boundaries by staying out and having premarital sex (we later discover that she is pregnant). These contentious issues are difficult for Enid to grapple with, and she observes this behaviour as a form of rebellion.

Context: Turn to page 26 to read more about the London youth culture of the time.

The tension escalates between mother and daughter in an argument about the secret Del has been keeping about losing her job. Del asserts herself, exclaiming: 'You can't talk to me like that. I'm not some kid' (page 33). This shows that the friction stems also from Del's need to assert her womanhood: she has come of age and is finding her place and identity in life.

Del is rebellious, which is characterised through her attempts at shoplifting. Enid confides in Mai that:

66 ENID. [...] Police, Miss Mai. She get a caution, but... the shame. (Scene Six, page 55)

Understandably Enid feels embarrassed at Del's conduct and worries that it calls her parenting into question. Perhaps Enid fears the judgement of the community, especially as she has raised the children on her own, and Del's delinquent behaviour is associated with unsupported parenting.

Del is assertive and wants others to know that she is confident in her identity. She states that 'I already know who I am' (page 20) when Mai attempts to read her palms. She feels suffocated by her mother, and speculates that she is keeping close surveillance over her:

> 66 DEL. […] I see you watching my stomach, making what you think are discreet enquiries about my periods. (Scene One, page 22)

Del and Mai become interdependent

The relationship between Mai and Del develops into a parent-child relationship. Both have biological parent-child relationships that are lost or damaged – Del's with Enid, and Mai's with her son – which perhaps draws them to one another to replace those figures in their lives.

Del is dyslexic

Del suffers with dyslexia and has been unsupported, creating barriers to her learning and a lack of confidence. Mai's reading of Del reveals this:

> 66 MAI. […] You have a liking for books, but when you read words run across the page like black ants. (Scene Five, page 47)

> 💡 **Task:** Research the effects of dyslexia.

Del's relationship with her sister Viv is important

Del has a close relationship with her sister and demands that she succeeds in her education, fulfilling their mother's desires. Del recognises the disappointment she is to her mother and equally basks in her sister's success. She reminds her of the perils of not completing her exams in Scene Five: 'And where's walking out gonna get you? A job in a factory?' (page 53). She warns her against messing her life up and insists that she completes her exams, which shows that Del is becoming wise and feels fiercely protective of Viv. Del recognises the opportunities that education affords a young Black woman in the 1980s when there is still widespread discrimination and prejudice. Education is a key to success and a means to climb up the social ladder.

Del's character development

Towards the end of the play, Del reveals that she is in fact pregnant, and has chosen to raise the baby independently from its father: 'For God's sake, Viv. He begged me, actually, but I weren't having none of it.' (page 51) She insists that he shouldn't have access to her or know where she lives: 'You better not have told him where I am.' (page 51). Perhaps because of her mother's grit in raising two children independently, Del doesn't fear the possibility of raising a baby on her own. She comes from a legacy of women who have suffered hardship, endured and survived. She is strong-willed, however she is also young and perhaps a bit naive.

At the end of the play, there is a lingering question about Enid's love for Del, and it seems that she wonders about the way her mother has loved her. Perhaps because of the barriers that Enid has created to protect herself, Del doesn't recognise her mother's love. However, it is clear in Enid's concluding **monologue** that she does in fact love Del: 'I would chop off my hand if it would help you' (page 72). Her own fight for survival has meant that she hasn't been able to be affectionate in the way that Del would hope. There is hope at the end of the play that perhaps Del will be able to break this generational trauma in connecting with her mother and through the mothering of her own child.

Viv

How does Pinnock present the character of Viv?

Characteristics:

- Studious
- Caring
- Ambitious/successful
- Intuitive
- Anxious

What does Viv represent?

- The second-generation Black British experience
- A mediator

Viv is younger than Del, at seventeen, and is about to take her A Levels. She is studious, hard-working and caring. Viv is her mother's pride and joy because of her academic successes and aspirations, as suggested by Enid boasting 'All 'A's.

My daughter going to university.' (page 28) She also acts as a mediator in the conflicts between Enid and Del.

Viv identifies as Caribbean and acknowledges her African heritage

In Scene One, it is clear that Viv has a natural curiosity about obeah. Mai and Brod give her a better understanding of who Enid is. This encourages Viv to delve deeper into her missing heritage, and creates a desire for her to visit Jamaica and give up her studies. As Broderick tells her stories of Jamaica and her African heritage, we see Viv contrasting this with her schooling, and yearning to make connections in order to flesh out her identity.

Viv is a mediator

Viv often defuses moments of tension between Enid and Del. They also both use her as their route to exchanging information. Enid verifies Del's job-loss through Viv, and Del enquires about her mother when she moves out.

Viv keeps Del's secrets. In Scene Two when Enid questions Del's late nights and work ethic, Viv covers for her sister:

> VIV. Don't you believe me?
>
> ENID. I was just wondering how she go to work in a place that give her the sack two week ago. [...]
>
> VIV. Promise me you're not going to make a scene. (page 25)

Alongside her efforts to keep the peace, Viv has a deep affection for her mother and empathises with the sacrifices that Enid has made.

Viv has a conflicting relationship with Enid

Viv jokes with Enid at the beginning of Scene Two, reciting Shakespeare while Enid is cleaning: 'Out, out damned spot' (page 24). This demonstrates their playful relationship, but also clearly shows the dynamic between them: Enid repeats the quotation with pride, as if Viv is the teacher and her mum the student. The **stage**

directions mark this moment: 'They share a smile before each resumes her work' (page 25).

Viv, however, feels the pressure to succeed and fulfil Enid's hopes for her, despite having ambitions of her own. She shares her hopes of visiting Jamaica with Brod in Scene Three: 'There's this volunteer programme. You go out there for a year and help out where they need you' (page 39). Clearly she has a deep desire to visit Jamaica, perhaps in order to connect with her identity.

Viv acknowledges that her mother works hard, and she feels undeserving of the sacrifices Enid has made:

> 66 VIV. She works so hard. I don't know how she does it. [...] How can I ever live up to that? We don't deserve it, Brod. (Scene Two, pages 30–31)

We can see how Viv struggles to forge her own path and feels guilty for wanting to do more than what Enid has planned for her.

Viv experiences feelings of unbelonging

Viv confides in Del that her teachers do not understand her. There is clearly a cultural barrier and Viv experiences a sense of disconnection:

> 66 VIV. Me and those teachers don't speak the same lingo. Things I feel they haven't got words for. I need another language to express myself.
> (Scene Five, page 53)

Viv feels stifled by the rigidity of the curriculum. She longs for an alternative outlet. Viv is defined by her academic successes at home but is humble enough to worry whether she will do well. She is insightful enough to recognise that she must seek other ways to define and validate who she is. Anxiety arises as she is uncertain how she will be accepted in her quest to redefine how others view her, particularly Enid.

Viv is Del's sister

Viv and Del are close, and she wants to be there for her sister. Both sisters encourage each other to strive for better. Del encourages Viv to maintain her studies after she walks out of one of her exams, and equally Viv wants to be a support for Del through her pregnancy:

> 66 VIV. How you gonna manage? [...] I'll help look after it if you come home.
> (Scene Five, page 51)

Even though Viv is concerned, she operates from a position of naivety, lacking the experience or wisdom to advise Del. While both sisters have grown up in the same environment, they have been affected differently by their circumstances. Viv has the privilege and access to education that Del does not, which affords her a different perspective.

Viv's character development

Throughout the play, we see Viv grapple with ideas about her identity. She enquires about Jamaica often, and in Scene Seven, highlights that Mooma was 'the last of our grandparents' (page 52). She feels a sense of loss and is clearly impacted by the displacement of her heritage. She isn't able to get the answers she is looking for through the curriculum in the secondary education system, and ultimately makes the choice to better understand who she is by reading Black Studies at university.

Mai

How does Pinnock present the character of Mai?

Characteristics:
- Gifted
- Wise
- Understanding
- Motherly
- Optimistic

What does Mai represent?

- A caregiver
- An adviser
- A healer
- A counsellor
- The **Windrush generation**
- Tradition
- Heritage and culture

Mai represents connections to African spirituality through her practice of obeah. Others depend on her and she fulfils several roles: caregiver, advisor, healer and counsellor. We first meet Mai in the **exposition** at the beginning of the play. Enid visits her to seek advice and wisdom about her mother's illness and Del's adolescent behaviour. The **stage directions** give us insights into Mai's lifestyle:

> *Keyword:*
> **Exposition** – where key information about characters and context is established.

66 MAI's bedsit. Very messy. The table centre stage is covered in papers, playing cards scattered all over, a glass of water and the remains of a half-burnt white candle. [...] MAI [...] wears a cardigan over her dress. She's slumped in the armchair, drinking from a bottle of stout. (page 13)

The audience is given the impression that Mai is burnt out and frustrated. Her slumped body language suggests that Mai is tired. Her gesture of throwing down the pen implies frustration. Her opening line in the play: 'Lord, see my troubles now' implies that something heavy is burdening her, something that she does not have the power to control or change, hence the need to call on a higher power to intercept. Like Enid, Mai forms part of the **Windrush generation**.

Mai's cultural background means that she identifies with Enid. She understands the perils of migration and the responsibility to send money back home. In Scene One, she advises Enid to 'send them what them ask for. You mother could do with it anyway' (page 20). Like Enid, she has made sacrifices in order to ensure that things are easier for the next generation: 'I was hard on my boy. I didn't hate him. I was trying to save him' (page 57). As a first-generation migrant, Mai is all too aware of the hardship of being Black and a woman, and perhaps tried to prepare her son for the difficulties that lay ahead of him by being 'hard' on him.

> *Context:* Turn to page 20 for more detail about migrants' experiences of racism and hardship.

Mai has experienced a lot of loss in her life

Mai has suffered multiple losses throughout her life, beginning with her mother. She shares her experience with Enid in Scene Six:

❝ MAI. So did mine. Eighteen years ago now. I still miss her. We don't appreciate them till them gone. (Scene Six, page 55)

The loss has deeply impacted Mai and she still grieves, indicating to Enid that the loss of Mooma will take time to process.

Mai was also married. We learn of her husband's passing in Scene Five, when Del asks: 'Do you ever talk to him… his spirit?' (page 46) Mai maintains a level of privacy, refusing to disclose whether or not she does talk to his spirit. It seems Mai is of an age where many of her friends and acquaintances have also passed. In Scene Eight she tells Del:

❝ MAI. I'm going to visit a friend a mine. Make a change to visit a friend in her living room rather than a cemetery. (page 69)

There is also loss in the estrangement between Mai and her son, which has left a void in her life that she attempts to fill, perhaps, with Del.

Mai is a motherly figure for Del

Mai connects with Del in their first encounter in Scene One, despite Del's resistance and dismissive attitude. Mai offers Del an olive branch:

❝ MAI. I can see you need to talk. (page 23)

In Scene Five, Del jokes that Mai enjoys her company:

❝ DEL. You like having me around. At first you thought I was a bit of a handful, but now you're starting to think that I'm actually quite good company. (*Imitating* MAI.) If me wrong say me wrong. (page 49)

Mai ultimately helps to restore the relationship between Del and Enid, reuniting them under a false guise (setting up a first client for Del, who turns out to be Enid).

Turn to page 100 to read more about the relationship between Mai and Del.

Mai represents a displaced people

Mai sums up the experiences of her generation and her ancestors. There is a sense of constant **unbelonging**:

> 66 MAI. [...] My grandfather's grandfather come to Jamaica in the hold of a ship. My mother did run away to Cuba in the twenties to cut cane, and I came here. It must be some kinda curse that condemn our people to wander the earth like ghosts who can't find rest. (Scene Six, page 58)

Mai insightfully expresses the feelings of the new generation, and the urge to feel welcomed and settled.

Mai is a practising obeah woman

Mai is an obeah woman, gifted with the talent to delve into a spiritual realm. However, she is burdened by her abilities and states in Scene One that 'Since I was thirteen I ain't had a moment's peace' (page 14).

Mai is frustrated by the demands of her clients, who seem to want to use her gift for personal gain:

> 66 MAI. These days people does just want me to help them win on the Mirror Bingo. [...] Is people I deal in. (Scene One, page 14)

Mai is only concerned with helping people, and values the importance of connection before she does a reading.

It is important for Mai to leave a legacy, and she recognises the gift in Del. She uses her time with her to hone Del's abilities and skills. In Scene Eight she references Del's training: 'Haven't you been watching me, listening to my consultations, reading my books?' (page 66) She has nurtured Del, sharing practices and traditions, such as Pocomania, in hope of sharing her legacy.

> **What is Pocomania?**
>
> Pocomania is a Jamaican folk religion stemming from African traditions, which combines revivalism and elements of Christianity.

Through Del's reading, the audience also discovers that Mai is unwell:

> 66 DEL. But what I saw...
>
> MAI. Never mind what you saw.
>
> DEL. Shouldn't you see a doctor?
>
> MAI. I don't need no doctor. What doctor know about a black woman soul? (Scene Eight, page 68)

There is a selfless element to Mai's character – she does not want to focus on herself, accepting that what will be will be. However, quoting Enid in Scene Six, she alludes to a mistrust of doctors and their ability to relate to her as a Black woman.

Mai's character development

Mai's last lines in the play, 'Remember, the healing begins when you look into their eyes. You can do it.' (page 70) are indicative of her character's journey. Her role is cyclical – the audience are introduced to Mai as a healer at the start of the play and by the end her healing is complete, as she restores the relationship between Del and Enid. Meanwhile we have learned that she may perhaps not be long for this world, but she has replaced herself as healer, and her role in the community, by training Del to take her place.

✏ **Playwright insight:**

'The play shows women caring for each other, women just looking out for each other, and understanding each other's predicament and helping each other.

When you think about feminism, that must be part of it: women valuing each other and validating each other. I always liked that it was called a sisterhood. And I like, at the end, that Del takes Mai's place in that role and that she comes into herself. Even though Del is written off, Mai sees her power and takes her under her wing.'

Broderick

How does Pinnock present the character of Broderick?

Characteristics:

- A proud Jamaican
- A heavy drinker

What does Brod represent?

- A father figure
- An archive of history
- The Black male experience
- The **Windrush generation**
- A window into Enid's past life

Broderick is the only male character in this female-centred play. His character performs an important literary purpose as a window into Enid's past life. He has an extremely close relationship with Enid stemming from their childhood in Jamaica. We assume that he was raised in close proximity to her family, as he references Mooma being like a mother to him too. He has witnessed Enid's relationships with her Mooma and her husband, and has seen how Enid raises Del and Viv. Broderick therefore offers important contextual information about all the characters' circumstances.

We first meet Brod in Scene Two, requesting Enid's help with securing his tie, and the audience are given an impression of the intimacy of their friendship.

Brod doesn't feel like a secure British National

As the conversation progresses in Scene Two, the audience is given insight into key historical moments that have shaped Brod, as well as his lived experience. He alludes to the Immigration Act of 1971:

66 BROD. [...] All my life I think of meself as a British subject, wave a flag on Empire Day, touch me hat whenever me see a picture a the queen. Then them send me letter say if me don't get me nationality paper in order they going kick me outta the country. (Scene Two, page 27)

Why is the immigration act of 1971 important?

It was implemented to limit the right to enter and live in the UK. It was created to stop permanent migration of people from the **Commonwealth** (this related mainly to Caribbeans and African nations). It meant that all Commonwealth citizens lost their automatic right to stay. You could only stay if you had lived in the UK for over five years or had a parent born in the UK. In order to live in the UK, you would need to have nationalisation documents or a British passport as proof of your status.

Context: For a more in-depth explanation, turn to page 17.

Context: Turn to page 19 for contextual information about the hostile environment in which migrants lived at this time.

Like Enid, Brod's education and understanding of England centred around the notion of being British. Brod was subject to discrimination and observed the vile behaviour of racists who violated the property of his friend Gullyman. In Scene Two, Brod speaks of the impact of racism. Gullyman's mental health has suffered and Brod says 'him mind crack' suggesting that Gullyman had a mental breakdown. We get the impression that this has deeply affected Brod, and he retells the story as if it haunts him.

Brod is a proud Jamaican

Due to the hostile environment, Brod clings to his Caribbean heritage. Compounded by the rejections and discrimination of the British, he finds his identity in the land where he was born. A *proud Jamaican*, he insists that Enid should teach her girls about their Caribbean roots:

> BROD. You teaching these children all wrong. They going forget where them come from. These girls ain't English like them newsreader who got English stamp on them like the letters on a stick a rock, right through English. These girls got Caribbean souls. (Scene Two, page 29)

Context: Turn to page 13 for more detail about Caribbean history.

Brod is a portal for Caribbean history. He teaches Del and Viv about the Maroons and slave revolts in Jamaica – he explains that they are descendants of strong warrior women who have overcome unthinkable hardships.

❝ BROD. [...] You, my dear, are descended from Queen Nanny. (Scene Two, page 29)

Perhaps Brod does this to instil a sense of pride and identity in the young girls. Brod uses the **oral tradition** to retell this historical narrative, a long-standing method of historical record-keeping common to Caribbean and African people.

> 💡 **Task:** Research oral tradition. You can begin with:
>
> rightforeducation.org/2018/07/04/the-rich-history-of-oral-tradition-in-africa
>
> There is also more on this subject on page 59 of this study guide.

Brod is perhaps a functioning alcoholic

Brod seems to drink quite heavily and is often holding or asking for an alcoholic drink:

❝ ENID. This is a map a your life, Brod: wine stain, Guinness, brandy...

BROD. Poor man not suppose to be sober, Enid. (Scene Two, page 26)

When he says 'Last time I sober me think me dead an' gone a hell' (page 26), it suggests that perhaps Brod uses alcohol as a coping mechanism to numb the pain that he has suffered. We discover in Scene Seven that Brod had a family:

❝ BROD. I didn't run away. Yes, I went wild for a time, when we was all young. I made mistakes but that didn't give her the right to say I couldn't see my kids, take them back to Jamaica. I yearn for them every day. (page 62)

Brod alludes to unfaithfulness and pines for his family, which in turn contributes to his drinking problem.

❝ BROD. Secure what? Till them change them mind again? 'This is my home.' (*Kisses his teeth*.) (page 28)

> *Key phrase:* **Kissing teeth** is a Caribbean expression of annoyance which involves sucking air through the teeth behind pursed lips.

Brod is a window into Enid's life before the play

We learn through Brod's dialogue that Enid's husband was abusive towards her, and that this was why she left him. Like Gullyman, Enid's husband is referred to as having a mental health condition – Brod calls him a 'madman' with an 'empty' look in his eyes (page 62). It seems as though the relationship between Enid and her husband was originally one of equality where they shared 'everything' and worked as a team. The change in his demeanour was ignited by the onslaught of racial abuse that he and Brod experienced at work:

66 BROD. It wasn't till we get job a Smithfield meat market that him start to change. Hear the other men, yah, 'Show us yer tail, yer black monkey.' Keep our mouth shut, keep our anger inside. (page 62)

Brod expresses the feelings of repression and being persecuted, and the toll this takes. Enid's husband projected the hate he experienced onto his wife:

66 BROD. [...] him come home from work bitter and tired [...] He want to wipe the smile off her face. (page 62)

Thus, through Brod we also learn about the male experience of racism in the 1970s and the impact it had on the mental health of Black men, resulting in the breakdown of families and of their own ability to function. Brod offers us a window into these experiences that become barriers to love and life.

Brod's character development

Brod's character offers the audience an insight into the Black male's struggle to **assimilate** and belong in the UK during the Windrush era. Alcohol is a coping mechanism through which he numbs himself, to drown out the sorrows of losing his family. It also becomes clear that Enid and the girls have become Brod's family in the absence of his own. In Scene Seven, Enid has thrown Brod out, saying she 'carry too many people for too long' (page 59). Brod drinks a bottle of rum to himself and considers serenading Enid under her window to regain his regular place at her dinner table.

'I feel very lucky to have been born when I was, and to be the child of that generation of people who first came over in the fifties. It was interesting to observe people making their lives here in those early days, and the community as it was then, because it was smaller and it was a community, and men were part of that. Even though there were a few families that were fractured, men were an important part of that community: father, uncles, brother. There were men like Brod I remember from my childhood, and one in particular who was a family friend who did have a problem with alcohol. I only have very vague memories now, but think I was drawing on that.

The vulnerabilities of people who come to this country are something I was particularly interested in, and you see that in Brod. But even with that vulnerability, I like the fact that Brod is so supportive of those women. There are men like Brod that are the "uncles" of a family, who have facilitated the growth and means to survive of the other members of that family. Despite them inhabiting these negative roles, and despite their obvious suffering, they might be allowing someone else to thrive. They might be supporting the growth of another person.'

Mooma

How does Pinnock present the character of Mooma?

Characteristics:
- Hardworking
- Determined

What does Mooma represent?
- A matriarch
- A survivor
- The struggle of life in Jamaica

Why is Mooma a significant character?

Although not physically present in the play, Mooma is an important figure in shaping Enid's character. As matriarch of the family, her treatment of Enid establishes the foundations of how Enid perceives herself. One could argue that Enid is unable to recognise the love that her mother had for her. At several junctures in the play she references the lack of love or connection she felt from Mooma:

66 ENID. Mooma never like me. I was everything she never want to be [...]
   (Scene Eight, page 72)

Mooma struggled to raise her family

There is no mention of Enid's father in the play, and we understand that the family lived in abject poverty. It seems as though Mooma was often away from home, working in the field.

66 ENID. [...] working hard like it was jus' any other day, cutting away with she cutlass. (Scene Four, page 43)

Enid is an example of a generation of women who were raised by mothers on the cusp of survival – who come from 'hard' love. Mooma demonstrated her love for her children through her role as provider. Day to day life would not have afforded mothers like Mooma time to spend with their children and nurture them. The primary focus would have been on providing for the family.

Turn to pages 31 and 66–68 to read about how Mooma responds to Enid's departure from Jamaica, and why she might respond that way. See also what Winsome Pinnock says about Mooma in the playwright insight on page 89.

Mooma's interaction with her children stems from the legacy of slavery, whereby mothers had to work in the field, often leaving their children with other carers, or to care for themselves. The fear of losing their children to be sold on to other plantations often led to mothers downplaying their children's qualities, to prevent them being desirable and taken away from them. The suppression of feelings was also cultivated, because people were unable to speak out against their treatment. These behaviours have become embedded into culture and passed down to later generations, and it is arguable that we see this in Mooma's relationship with Enid.

Dr Joy DeGruy's work examines the legacy of slavery, and she argues that certain learned behaviour has been inscribed in the psyches of the descendants of enslaved people. You can read more about this in her book: *Post Traumatic Slave Syndrome*.

How has Mooma shaped Enid as a mother?

What is clear is that Mooma's parenting has affected Enid's own parenting style. Mooma's upbringing provided Enid with structure, routine, values, morals and tradition, but not openness or overt affection. There are echoes of their relationship in that between Enid and Del. Del's own departure from Enid echoes that of Enid's departure from Mooma – there is no goodbye. Del also questions Enid's love for her.

Mooma very likely had the same hopes and dreams that Enid has for her girls, and that Del will have for her own child. Mooma underpins what Enid came from and gives us insight into the difficulties Caribbean peoples suffered in poverty in their native countries, which spurred them to take up the opportunity to leave for the UK.

How Mooma's death helps us to understand the development of Enid's character

Mooma's death acts as a turning point for Enid's understanding of herself and her daughters. The conversations she has throughout the play concerning Jamaica, and then her mother's death, lead her to reflect on the relationship she had with Mooma. Her feeling of being unloved is expressed most clearly at the end of the play:

66 ENID. [...] I want someone to tell me stories to make the sun shine, someone to gather... gather me up and touch my cheek like I was a prize, not a curse, and stroke my hair like Mooma never could. (Scene Eight, page 72)

We understand that Enid has battled with feelings of rejection and has suppressed and hidden those feelings. Losing her mother has made her vulnerable, and almost like a child again. She yearns for that protection, perhaps knowing that it cannot be recovered now that Mooma had passed.

How to write about characters

Here are some useful things to consider as you revise, make notes and write responses to do with characters:

- Describe and assess the character's role in the play.

- What motivates them?

- What do we learn from their relationships and communication with other characters?

- How does the character use language?

- What do others say about them?

- What lessons do we learn from this character?

- How does the context influence the way they behave?

- What are the main lessons your character has learned by the end of the play?

- What are the central themes surrounding your character?

Example exam question

On some exam boards (ask your teacher for guidance), questions can focus on a particular character and how their portrayal helps to explore a theme. For example:

How does Pinnock use the character of Enid to explore the theme of identity and belonging in *Leave Taking*?

Write about:

- How Enid is presented as at different points in the play.

- How Pinnock conveys ideas about identity and belonging.

Here is an example of a paragraph structured using the 'Point, Evidence, Analysis' technique, as part of a response to this question:

> 1. Put your quotations in context to show where they fit in to the play.

[Point] Over a lengthy period of time in the UK, Enid has assimilated and forged a British identity, and seems to feel a sense of belonging. **[Evidence]** In Scene Two, in conversation with Brod about migrating to England and visiting 'back home', she says[1] 'why you nuh go back there you have such a longing for it? I don't dream about going back home because this is my home.' [*Analysis*] She is both challenging and dismissive of Brod with her rhetorical question, and she asserts that she does not 'dream about going back home', as though it has become a distant memory. Through the use of the possessive pronoun 'my'[2] Pinnock suggests that Enid has established a sense of belonging. Perhaps this sense of belonging also derives from the lengthy process of nationalisation that Enid had to go through in order to become a British citizen.[3]

> 2. Go into detail about individual words and phrases in your quotation: use technical terms and explain why the playwright's choice is effective.

> 3. Include historical context to demonstrate your understanding of the world of the play and its characters.

To write a full essay, you would also need an introduction, more paragraphs, and a conclusion. There are lots of tips to help you with this in the chapter Essay Questions and How to Answer Them from page 145.

Themes

Identity, belonging, racism and prejudice

At its core, *Leave Taking* is about the British immigrant experience. Pinnock explores how ideas about identity and belonging, and racism, impact each of the characters.

There is a clear divide and built-in tension between the Windrush generation and their children, so we'll explore these two generations' experiences separately:

The Windrush generation

Mai, Enid and Broderick received education and mythology about the '**Mother Country**' (the UK) and how it would offer opportunities superior to those in Jamaica. Broderick represents the rude awakening many immigrants received on discovering that they were not welcomed. Whilst he has continued to make his life in Britain, he is pragmatic and under no illusions.

Context: Turn to page 14 to read more on this topic.

Enid reveals positive memories of Jamaica in Scenes Five and Eight, reflecting on the community and the sharing of resources that took place in order to get by. In the UK, Enid talks of being alone, and how one has to fend for oneself and live with the consequences. This links to the racism, hostility and **othering** that has become part of her daily life. Del's retelling of Enid's mistreatment at a staff party speaks of the way Black people were demeaned, and the trauma this creates for their British-born children. We see Enid almost willing to sacrifice herself in order for her children to buy into Britishness.

Enid believes that hard work, playing by the rules, and being British-born will lead to acceptance for herself and her children. She casts off many of the happier memories of being in Jamaica in order to justify the life she is leading in the UK.

Through Enid, Pinnock depicts the reluctance of the Windrush generation to speak of their experiences both back home and on coming to Britain.

Being able to turn to both the church and to Mai are important to Enid. Mai represents a bridge between Africa, the Caribbean and the UK in her role as an obeah woman: the space this tradition occupied within communities in the Caribbean is transported to the UK. It is important to Mai that the tradition continues, as seen in her talent-spotting of Del.

Broderick symbolises what it means to be proud of your roots. He dreams wistfully of Jamaica and shares it with the girls, talking of them having 'Caribbean souls', and he is keen for them to stay connected to this heritage. There is very little of his experience in the UK that shows him that any degree of compliance or assimilation will give him equal rights. He is prepared to speak up about inequalities, and his experiences have contextual relevance for audiences today in the wake of the Windrush scandal.

Windrush children

Through Del and Viv, Pinnock depicts how the second generation navigate life as British-born people with direct heritage to Jamaica. We learn that Enid tells them very little about their background, imploring them to 'forget about Jamaica' (page 39), and it is clear that they have never visited.

Context: Turn to page 28 to read more on this topic.

Del's experience of education mirrors the prejudiced attitude many schools had towards Black children, and it is likely that Del has dyslexia. She references the racial tensions present in Britain at the time, and has become closely connected to the emerging Black British cultural scene.

Context: Turn to pages 24 and 26 to read more on these topics.

Viv seems more tolerant, immersing herself in literature and her studies. She is presented as a buffer between her mother and Del, but eventually realises that she herself has no idea who she is or where she fits. She comes to understand Del more through sharing this experience, however, **ironically**, Del believes, like Enid, that Viv has more of a chance by conforming, and insists that education will be empowering.

Key quotations: Identity, belonging, racism and prejudice

ENID. I don't dream about back home because this is my home. (Scene Two, page 27)	Enid's **possessive pronoun** 'my' shows how she is determined to make Britain her home regardless of the difficulties.
BROD. Me, I dream about the land a wood and water. Pure rainforest. (Scene Two, page 27)	Broderick's romantic depiction of the landscape of Jamaica highlights his wistful feelings about the country of his birth, and contrasts with Enid's descriptions.
BROD. All my life I think of myself as a British subject, wave a flag on Empire day, touch me hat whenever me see a picture of the queen. (Scene Two, page 27)	Broderick's **tone** of indignation and betrayal indicates that he believes his compliance was wasted.
BROD. Nanny, an Ashanti warrior queen, a powerful woman, becomes their leader. (Scene Two, page 29)	Broderick is keen for the girls to be infused with the power and triumph of their predecessors, and uses vocabulary associated with strength: 'warrior', 'queen', 'powerful' and 'leader', to reinforce this.
DEL. I been following that sound system for years. The bass is mad. You wanna see it pounding the walls, like one big pulsing heart. (Scene Two, page 33)	Del finds expression and belonging by joining the Black London music scene. The **simile** of 'one big pulsing heart' illustrates her need to feel connected and in harmony with her life and surroundings.
VIV. But no matter how hard I search for myself in them books, I'm never there. (Scene Five, page 53)	Viv demonstrates that it is harder to form a strong sense of identity when you do not see your own experiences reflected in what you study. She uses the **metaphorical** idea of searching for herself in books to express this.
ENID. In a way we poorer than them. Them all in it together. When I was a girl you kill a cow you share it up, everybody in the distric' get a piece. Here, you poor and you by yourself. (Scene Eight, page 71)	Enid demonstrates how she felt a sense of belonging in Jamaica, despite being very poor. She points to a sense of community and that in Britain her experience has been isolating. She uses **contrast** here to balance her description of these two experiences.

ENID. Nobody see you, nobody hear you. You could work fifty years with people and they still don't know you name. (Scene Eight, page 72)	Enid's **repetition** of 'nobody' emphasises how she feels invisible and dehumanised.
ENID. You don't exist. How you going teach you children that they don't exist? You got to show them how life hard. (Scene Eight, page 72)	Pinnock uses **paradox** in 'teach you children that they don't exist' to highlight the confusion of feeling alienated and invisible in society. Enid's **rhetorical question** conveys her sense of helplessness.

Education

Pinnock highlights the importance of formal education but also explores the lack of it, and the importance of life lessons and training.

Academic excellence

Many immigrant groups believe that education will be a way out of poverty and a way to integrate and be respected by society. Pinnock depicts this through Enid, who reassures herself that her decision to come to the UK will be beneficial to Viv and Del. She firmly believes that education will bring the girls respect and acceptance, and does not seem to view knowing about their history, origins and identity as a relevant part of that education. Enid is impressed by what Viv is learning and shows favour to Viv, deliberately saving for her future in education. Viv is clearly motivated by Enid's view on education but worries about disappointing her.

Special educational needs

Where Viv sails through her exams, Del struggles, largely it would seem due to dyslexia. We only discover this when Mai performs an impromptu reading. Del enjoys reading but the struggles and lack of support for her special needs means that she is unable to engage. She is outspoken and brash, but underneath this lies the frustration and difficulty she experiences with education. She masks her struggles with anger, suspicion and by connecting with her peers through music outside of school.

However, Del still values education. We know this because Del champions Viv's success and is adamant that Viv completes her exams. Enid has been successful in instilling the importance of education as a gateway to success.

Disaffection

Pinnock shows how both Viv and Del become disaffected and frustrated by their education. Del leaves school early and without qualifications, which affects her job prospects. It could be argued that the education system has failed her. Viv relates to Del's experiences because whilst her academic success is validated, she does not feel recognised or affirmed as a person. She expresses that the content of the curriculum does not feel inclusive of her culture. Her story and experiences do not seem to be reflected in her education. She decides that she needs to know more about herself and her heritage, and realises that this will not be taught either by her school or by Enid. Whilst there is a tense moment in Scene Five when Viv has walked out of an exam, by the end of the play she has found a way to move forward, and to pursue her interest in her own culture and heritage through the university degree Enid wanted for her.

Being self-taught, life experiences and apprenticeship

Broderick has learned both from his life experiences and by reading about Jamaican history. He has learned from the failure of his marriage, and Enid's, and his attempts to be a decent father figure to the girls. He has learned a profound life lesson through the tale of Gullyman: Broderick employs the **oral tradition** of storytelling to unpack the meaning of the story. For him, Gullyman's story is an **allegory**, warning of the adverse effects living in a hostile country can have on one's mental health.

> Keyword: an **allegory** is a story with a hidden (typically moral or political) meaning.

Del is resistant to Mai and her practices at the start of the play, but later pursues an informal apprenticeship with Mai, which allows her to find peace, validation and her gift. Pinnock shows how Del places herself within a continuum and tradition, giving her hope for the future.

There is a sense of coming full circle, and even **irony**, as Enid's quest for a better life for her children in Britain leads to both of them leaning into their Jamaican culture and traditions, in order to forge a meaningful life in the UK.

Key quotations: Academic excellence

ENID. All 'A's. My daughter going to university. How many a my sister children back home going to university? (Scene Two, page 28)	Viv's academic success is a source of pride to Enid, and she sees it as proof that her move to the UK has been beneficial to her girls. She reinforces this belief with her **rhetorical question**.
VIV. And what if I fail my exams? What'll she do then? (Scene Two, page 31)	The **pronoun** in Viv's question: 'What'll she do?', rather than 'What'll I do?' emphasises how Viv's need for academic success is more for her mother than herself. Viv is aware of the sacrifices Enid made for Viv's British education, and fear of letting her mother down is a source of stress as she prepares for her A levels.
DEL. Are you trying to fuck your life up? Get out. (Scene Five, page 53)	Del's **expletive** and the **imperative** 'Get out' combine to create a confrontational **tone** that reinforces the values around education that Enid has imparted. Whilst Del has other interests and is more aligned with the youth culture of the time, she is still keen for Viv to conform.

Key quotations: Special educational needs

MAI. You have a liking for books, but when you read words run across the page like black ants. (Scene Five, page 47)	Pinnock employs a **simile** in Mai's reading of Del, and the visual **imagery** helps the audience to understand Del's experience, giving a sense of the words being hard to pin down.
MAI. The teachers say you slow [...] (Scene Five, page 47)	The teachers' idea that Del is 'slow' is dismissive in its **tone**, and **contrasts** with the care, attention and understanding offered by Mai.

Key quotations: Disaffection

DEL. But what you give us that we can use out there? You don't see the police vans hunting us down [...] (Scene Three, page 34)	Del is frustrated by the feeling that Enid's approach to educating her girls has not taught them tools that are applicable in their everyday life. Her frustration is emphasised by her **rhetorical question**.
VIV. But no matter how hard I search for myself in them books, I'm never there. (Scene Five, page 53)	Viv's **metaphor** of looking for herself emphasises how all the knowledge she has acquired still leaves questions about her own identity unanswered.
ENID. Black Studies. You ever hear of such a thing? (Scene Eight, page 71)	Enid's **question** shows her seeking validation for her own uncertainty – also conveyed through the **short sentence** 'Black Studies'. Compare this with her immediate and confident approval when Viv recites from her literature studies in Scene Two.

Key quotations: Being self-taught, life experiences and apprenticeship

BROD. Gullyman heart brock, him mind crack, and now he can hardly talk broken English. (Scene Two, page 29)	The **conclusion** of Brod's Gullyman **allegory** operates as a warning and a life lesson.
BROD. You, my dear, are descended from Queen Nanny. [...] Is in the blood. Thas why Black woman so strong. (Scene Two, page 29)	Brod is speaking **metaphorically** here, as the girls may not literally be descended from Queen Nanny, however he wishes to convey to them how a greater sense of their cultural and genetic heritage and identity should make them feel strong.

Family

Ideas about family are also presented in a many-layered way by Pinnock, who explores immediate family, extended family, broken families, and the new families we choose for ourselves: our friends.

Immediate family

At the start of the play, we are introduced to Enid as a single parent with two teenage daughters. She says 'I have to be man and woman' (Scene Six, page 55), and there are clear indications throughout the play that Enid wanted a more conventional **'nuclear' family**. She was married, and had hopes and dreams about what her family would look like, which have not come true. It is clear that having to play both roles has been a struggle for Enid, with all decision-making left to her. Pinnock cleverly portrays Enid's strength and determination as well as her doubts as she negotiates the perils of parenting through successes and difficulties.

> *Keyword:* A **nuclear family** is the traditional family unit of a mother, father and their children.

Extended family

Pinnock also shows how an extended family can look and the challenges this extension can create.

Many Caribbeans, like other migrants, found themselves having to leave behind parents, children, partners, grandparents, cousins, siblings and so on, in order to seek a 'better' life abroad. When **nuclear families** were split up by migration, there was often an understanding that others would be 'sent for' once those in the UK got settled. We see this with Enid's husband sending her a ticket to join him after a year in the UK.

For many it was unlikely that they would send for family beyond that nucleus, and for Enid, Mai and Broderick it would seem that most of their extended family were left behind in Jamaica. Pinnock presents to us the varying levels of loneliness this creates, and for Brod his escape is in drink. Mai is also alone in her bedsit, and we see her trying to conjure a sense of home and family by recreating her backyard from Jamaica in London by keeping chickens.

The portrayal of Enid and her extended family highlights the strength of family ties and the sense of responsibility and obligation it brings. She has left behind her mother and siblings. Her sister constantly begs Enid to send money or other things, and she has to plan and save for visits home.

It was very common for many once established in the UK to return home for visits regularly, even yearly, and some sent their children back for summer holidays to connect with their extended families. However, in Enid's case, there has been a long interval since her last visit (five years), and Del and Viv have never visited. This might tell us that Enid has been unable to afford this expense in addition to having to provide for her family in the UK and back home.

New family: friends

Pinnock also explores the way in which new 'families' are formed. Enid doesn't seem to have any other family in the UK and her only friend, Broderick, is from childhood. Pinnock's characterisation of Broderick represents the way that Caribbeans extended their families beyond blood ties, out of necessity and a need to bond and replace those who were left behind. Broderick is presented as a friend of the family, but also as a father figure: in Scene Two, Enid asks him 'You read Viv school report?' (page 28). The girls call him 'Brod' and more affectionately and traditionally (in line with Caribbean etiquette), 'Uncle Brod', and he is a regular fixture in Enid's household. Del explains that he 'lives up the road from us and stops by every day for his rice and peas' (Scene Seven, page 59).

Many Windrush migrants travelled alone and welcomed the opportunity to bond with others in their situation. They often found themselves in houses divided into bedsits, living alongside others in similar situations: dilapidated multiple dwellings were often the only accommodation they could come by due to racism and prejudice. Mai's bedsit is representative of this reality. Through shared living arrangements, relationships were formed among people from across the varying Caribbean islands, and new 'aunties' and 'uncles' sprung from those relationships.

Enid, Broderick and Mai all represent examples of 'broken' families, being estranged from members of their original 'nucleus'. However, we see Mai and Del drawing close and building a new home together. Del is able to talk to Mai in a way she is unable to with Enid, and Mai obviously sees Del's potential. She is happy to listen to Del and is more successful in understanding Del's perspective than she was with her own son. Just as Del manages to find a more 'suitable' mother figure, she is also on the brink of creating yet another new family, with the birth of her own child.

Pinnock therefore explores two definitions of 'broken family', one rooted in the *separation* of families, through 'leave taking' (creating the physical barrier of country borders), and the other in the breakdown of family relationships.

Key quotations: Immediate family

ENID. We sit by we self and plan through the night. We going to be big shots in London. (Scene Five, page 44)	Enid's excitement is depicted in the idea of her planning with her husband 'through the night'.
ENID. Me husban' long gone, yes. But I don't want him back, I bring up those two girls on me own. (Scene One, page 17)	The phrase 'long gone' implies that Enid has got used to her situation and the responsibility she now has to shoulder alone.
BROD. I made mistakes but that didn't give her the right to say I couldn't see my kids, take them back to Jamaica. I yearn for them every day. (Scene Seven, page 62)	Broderick talks about loneliness and isolation through the loss of his **nuclear family** who returned to Jamaica. The intense 'yearning' he feels 'every day' shows the depth of his feelings.

Key quotations: Extended family

ENID. The woman so lie. I don't know whether to believe her or not. How I know she nah want the money for herself? (Scene One, page 18)	Pinnock shows Enid's confusion and distrust in the **contrast** between her first two sentences, as she moves between certainty and uncertainty that her sister is lying.

Key quotations: New families

DEL. There's loads to do round here. I'm in charge of them chickens. They've all got their own unique personalities. (Scene Five, page 51)	The relationship that Del builds with Mai includes her being given and maintaining responsibilities for the first time, which is empowering for Del, as demonstrated through the phrase 'I'm in charge'.

Hopes and aspirations

Pinnock contrasts the reality of being raised on a small tropical island, steeped in religion and spiritualism, deep poverty and colonialism, to life in the '**Mother Country**' where you are a minority, raising children who will be different to you. There is a sense of doom and foreboding, but somehow Pinnock shows that the aspirations of the Windrush generation are robust and not in vain. She reveals that even through adversity, hope and aspiration are key ways of lifting oneself out of poverty and hard times.

In Scene Five we learn about the dreams Enid had for her life in London. Enid seems to have given up on her own dreams, but she has hope and aspirations for her girls, and in particular Viv. She believes that in sacrificing her own dreams she has given her girls a better start than she received in Jamaica. Whilst Viv later questions her education, somehow she is able to find her own happiness and sense of the future by tailoring Enid's aspirations.

The run-down setting of Mai's bedsit and the girls' initial dismissal suggest that obeah is a dying form. However, Pinnock later presents hope and a continuation of this practice through Del. It is made to seem very unlikely at the start of Scene One that Del would by Scene Eight be starting her own career in obeah.

Whilst the play clearly tackles the relationships between two generations and the inevitable frictions this can cause, Pinnock is keen to offer hope here too. The characters all move towards a deeper understanding of each other, and help each other to do this:

Who helps whom?	Quotation	Analysis
Broderick encourages Del and Viv to connect with their heritage.	BROD. You, my dear, are descended from Queen Nanny. (Scene Two, page 29)	Pinnock conveys through Brod's **image** how the girls represent the future as well as the past.
Viv helps Enid.	VIV. I can make you some fried dumpling. (Scene Four, page 43)	Viv's offer **symbolises** how Enid has raised her children so that they will be able to help, support and comfort her.

Who helps whom?	Quotation	Analysis
Mai helps Del.	MAI. Look, you want to stay here in my house you abide by my rules, y'hear? You got to learn to respect... (Scene Five, page 47)	Mai uses the terms 'abide' and 'rules' to emphasise how discipline is important in pursuit of goals.
Del helps Mai.	DEL. You like having me around. At first you thought I was a bit of a handful, but now you're starting to think that I'm actually quite good company. (Scene Five, page 49)	This demonstrates how Del is able to take on responsibility and recognise her worth. The **metaphor** 'handful' shows Del's ability to be reflective about her behaviour.
Viv helps Del to understand their mother better.	DEL. You're her favourite. (Scene Five, page 52)	Del is in denial and fights against trying to understand Enid, too caught up in her own problems.
Mai helps Enid.	MAI. Nuttin. I give as a friend. (Scene Six, page 57)	Unlike in Scene One where Mai seeks money, by Scene Six a friendship is established and Mai wants to help.
Enid and Del reconcile.	[DEL] *joins* ENID *at the table and takes her mother's hand into both her own* [...] (Scene Eight, page 72)	This description serves as a powerful **image** of hope and the future as Enid now has a more meaningful relationship with Del.

Disillusionment

The other side of aspiration comes when hopes and dreams are dashed or severely challenged, and a person becomes disillusioned. Pinnock's exploration of disillusionment is linked to the wellbeing and mental health of the characters:

Del reveals how school and work make her feel subhuman. There is a feeling of helplessness and confusion in her characterisation.

Viv becomes disillusioned with education, even though she is arguably the only character to have found a way to **assimilate**. She learns that happiness is more than being academically successful and toeing the line.

Enid puts on a brave face and is optimistic for her girls in Scene Two, but by Scene Eight she is forced to admit that she is aware that the girls struggle, and her anger rises to the surface.

Broderick's experiences have led him to make sure he has a back-up plan in a possible return to Jamaica. He is strongly influenced by the story of his friend Gullyman, who finally gave up on trying to be more English than the English after he experienced racist abuse, and Brod saw the the toll this took on his mental health.

Pinnock shows how hope and disillusionment are both human conditions, and all characters veer between both.

Key quotations: Disillusionment

BROD. Secure what? Till them change them mind again? 'This is my home.' (*Kisses his teeth.*) I make sure me Jamaican passport up to date. An' you better do the same. (Scene Two, page 28)	Broderick's experience of finding that his nationality status is insecure makes him disillusioned with his British citizenship. He doesn't trust the authorities to continue to allow him to stay, and Pinnock emphasises this distrust with the stage direction '**kisses his teeth**'.
DEL. Grateful for what? This shithole? A greasy job in a greasy café where they treat me like a dum dum [...] (Scene Three, page 34)	The **noun** 'shithole' displays Del's anger, while the **adjective** 'greasy' shows how disgusted she is, and the **repetition** of it reinforces her frustration. *Keywords:* an **adjective** is a describing word for a **noun**.
BROD. Poor man not suppose to be sober, Enid. Last time I sober me think me dead an' gone a hell. (Scene Two, page 26)	Brod uses drink to escape. Through the **image** of being 'dead an' gone a hell', Pinnock presents to us how he feels about the reality of his life as a 'poor man'.

ENID. Sometime I feel like a cat chasing him own tail. Going round and getting nowhere but dizzy. (Scene Four, page 42)	When Enid's mother dies, the veneer finally cracks and Enid reveals her true longing for home and the toll that the cruelty and hostility has had on her. Note how Pinnock uses the **simile** 'like a cat' to **symbolise** Enid's despair at the futility of her life.
MAI. The teachers say you slow, so you give up and run with a crowd who make you feel like you belong. (Scene Five, page 47)	Del has a tough exterior, but Mai is able to cut through it, identifying how she feels underneath.
ENID. You say I don't see how them treat you out there. I see it. I see it and it make me want to tear the place down. (Scene Eight, page 72)	No longer putting on a brave face, by the end of the play, Enid admits that she sees the girls struggle in life, and her anger rises to the surface with her **repetition** of 'I see it' and violent **image** of 'tear[ing] the place down'.

Guilt and responsibility

Pinnock goes even deeper into negative emotions experienced by the characters, exploring ideas about guilt, but also shows how they take responsibility, and grow and learn from their experiences.

Mai feels guilty about the breakdown of her relationship with her son. She realises that she was unable to understand his struggle. The advice she gives to Enid comes from her own experience of raising her son, and she attempts to right those wrongs by advising Enid on what not to do. By listening to Del, offering shelter and allowing Del to feel that what young people are experiencing is valid, Mai is able to absolve herself of that guilt.

Enid, too, is racked by guilt for having left her mother and wider family in Jamaica to seek a new life in the UK. She works extremely hard but still struggles to provide the basics, which leaves her feeling very guilty about the little she has left to send back home.

Viv sees the sacrifices Enid has made for them, and is concerned that she will not fulfill her mother's dreams by going to university. She also recognises and feels guilty that her choice of pathway is far more acceptable to her mother and therefore she is prioritised over Del.

Del feels guilt as she believes that she has let her mother down by being rebellious and not succeeding academically.

Key quotations: Guilt and responsibility

ENID. I do my best, but every week me sister send another letter a beg me for this and a beg me for that. [...] She must think I'm living like a millionaire. (Scene One, page 19)	Enid left and gave up her family and home with the widely shared understanding that she would make good in the UK and lift them all up by sending money and resources back home, but she finds her best is never enough. Her frustration is clear in the **simile** 'like a millionaire'.
VIV. How can I ever live up to that? We don't deserve it, Brod. (Scene Two, page 31)	Viv is aware of the sacrifices that Enid has made and feels that she can't repay them. Her **rhetorical question** demonstrates her feelings of inadequacy and guilt.
MAI. I was hard on my boy. (Scene Six, page 57)	Mai acknowledges the fact that she was unable to understand and support her son. There is a **tone** of regret in her use of the word 'hard'.

Form, Structure and Language

All plays are written with the intention that they will be performed, and over time, a play's form and structure has developed around key ingredients. *Leave Taking* uses many of the tools used to craft any play, but Pinnock also deviates from the traditional structure. *Leave Taking* is very compact and precise, with the actual events taking place over four to six weeks in the 1980s. However, the central themes continue to be relevant to audiences right up to the present.

Form: Drama

Drama as a form has a number of conventions. The traditional contents of a play when written down are often as follows:

- Dramatis Personae (the character list) with some brief details, e.g. age or relationship to another character.

- Acts – dividing the play into two to five large sections. Within each act are a number of...

- Scenes – smaller segments of drama that are related and sit inside an act.

- Settings – locations, indicated by stage design such as scenery, lighting and sound.

- **Stage directions** – indicating everything from the appearance of the stage (where furniture or **props** are, descriptions of costumes or lighting) to the physical actions of the characters.

Pinnock, however, discards the structure of using acts altogether. The play is organised into eight scenes all taking place in either Enid's flat or Mai's bedsit. The use of scenes enables the story and its themes to unfold easily and with a momentum that adds to the overall dramatic effect. Some scenes are much longer than others as Pinnock expands on each of her themes and characters as needed.

Settings

Pinnock locates the play in London, but the roots of all the characters lie in Jamaica. The influence of both these cultures is visible in the play's settings.

Context: Turn to page 21 for detail about the living circumstances of the Windrush generation when they arrived in the UK.

Scene One, located at Mai's bedsit in Deptford, South London, introduces us to a quartet of women across two generations, two born in Jamaica and two in the UK. The use of the bedsit as a central location in the play points to the beginning of life in the UK for many of the **Windrush generation**.

We return to the bedsit for Scenes Six, Seven and Eight, where we see Del and Mai's relationship develop, as well as Del resolving her conflict with Enid. The use of the bedsit is **symbolic**, as even though it might imply that Mai is only temporarily settled, it provides great stability for all the characters because of Mai. It also symbolises the abilities of many Windrush people to create permanency in adverse circumstances and bring their culture to bear on their new lives in the UK.

So, the bedsit as a location serves many purposes:

- Mai's home.
- Mai's workplace.
- A place of sanctuary for others looking for meaning (Del, Enid).
- A cultural pitstop – links to back home.
- Del's home.
- Del's workplace.

Pinnock chooses Enid's flat on the Caledonian Road in North London as the second location. Many Caribbeans created community and supported each other to graduate from their bedsits, purchasing traditional terraced houses (many of which were in less sought-after areas and in need of repair). These homes usually had a front and back room downstairs, allowing for the use of a 'special' room, with great cultural value in the lives of Caribbeans as the place for socialising, entertaining and showing the best of what you have (e.g. ornaments) to your visitors. However, Enid does not have a dedicated 'front room' for 'best' as this is a flat. The commitment to keeping the living room scrupulously tidy and ordered is alluded to in Scene Two as Enid prepares for the pastor's visit. Enid's living room is a communal living space:

- Where Viv does her homework.

- Where Enid entertains guests.

- Where they eat.

- Where Enid sits alone at night with her thoughts and memories.

- Which acts as a family meeting place.

There are many ways that the play could be presented on stage, including the use of a dual set-up of the two locations. Pinnock's decision to write for just these two settings creates a sense of isolation, which is a theme throughout the play. There is also a sense of both locations being a sanctuary from the hostile outside world. An image is created of five adults existing in a very small and limited space, which adds to the tension each character experiences, and to the tension in the relationships between them.

> What **props** and details do you think are essential in creating both settings and how they are presented in each of the scenes?

Stage directions

The information provided in the **stage directions** gives clues about the characters' lives, relationships and feelings.

Each scene begins with a time marker, and states where it is taking place. There are also details about how the scene should look:

❝ MAI's bedsit. Very messy. The table centre stage is covered in papers, playing cards scattered all over, a glass of water and the remains of a half-burnt white candle. (page 13)

Pinnock is also concerned with the positioning of characters around the setting, letting us know variously that:

- Broderick is lying on the table (Scene Seven).

- Del is at the window looking at the chickens (Scene One).

- Viv is on the sofa, books on knees (Scene Two).

- Enid is sitting in the dark (Scene Four).

Through the stage directions, we also get an indication of how the characters are feeling at that moment, for example:

❝ ENID *seems distracted, lost.* (Scene Six, page 54)

Sound

Pinnock uses sound effectively throughout the play to evoke culture, and day-to-day living, as well as to create atmosphere and mood:

Chickens – Pinnock clearly introduces the sound of chickens in Scene One with the stage direction 'A cock crows' (page 21), and we are invited to be aware of them whenever the scenes are located at Mai's (until their disappearance in Scene Seven).

Music – Pinnock conjures the atmosphere of the eighties and prior, through music. The music becomes a vehicle for depicting the times, but also the characters and how they are feeling. Music is also used to differentiate between the two generations.

In Scene Three, Brod and Enid listen and dance to music that speaks to them and allows them to express joy and a sense of lightheartedness through the unease.

❝ BROD *puts a record on. It is heavy dub. He closes his eyes and feels the music.* ENID *taps her feet.* BROD *opens his eyes. He takes her hands and pulls her up. They both feel the heavy bass moving through them, dancing together at first then separately in their own worlds.* (page 31)

Context: To read more about sound system culture, turn to page 26.

In Scene Two, Del mentions the importance of music to her and her generation through the **sound systems**.

❝ DEL. All I did last night was dance. What's wrong with that? I like dancing. I been following that sound system for years. The bass is mad. You wanna see it pounding the walls, like one big pulsing heart. When that bass gets inside you and flings you round the room you can't do nothing to stop it. (Scene Two, page 33)

Structure: Time

Pinnock is quite clear in how she indicates both time passing and time of day, but a director would decide how aspects of time are shown to the audience through lighting, clothing, and the way the development of characters is portrayed.

Timeline

Overall, the play takes place over a few weeks, but the bulk of the action is actually condensed into a couple of specific days and evenings.

Scene	Timeline	Set	Who's in it
Scene One	The now...	Mai's bedsit	Mai, Enid Viv and Del
Scene Two	A few days later	Enid's living room	Enid, Viv, Brod and Del
Scene Three	A few hours later	Enid's living room	Enid, Viv and Brod
Scene Four	Late into that night	Darkness – Enid's living room	Viv and Enid
Scene Five	A few weeks later	Mai's room	Mai, Viv and Del
Scene Six	Evening	Mai's room	Mai, Enid and Del
Scene Seven	Very early the next morning	Mai's bedsit	Mai, Brod and Del
Scene Eight	A few weeks later	Mai's bedsit	Mai, Enid and Del

The final scene is a few weeks later, allowing enough time to have passed for the audience to see the development and reflection of the characters. But in reading or watching the play, the pace is fast and the growth of the characters is quite stark. In this time, Del becomes an adult and Mai's health deteriorates.

Timing

Each scene takes place in 'real time'. Whilst the characters allude to outside events and clearly things take place between scenes (such as the Pastor's visit), we are able to watch the characters as a particular aspect of their lives unfolds. We also get to experience their responses to external events, such as Del's relationship with her boss, and the parties she attends. The events that happen in between the scenes create momentum, making the focus of each scene more believable to the audience. They also allow Pinnock to cover much more ground and create very rounded characters.

Broader passage of time

Whilst the play homes in on just five characters over a few weeks, descriptions of the broader passage of time allow more characters to be introduced to us, such as Gullyman and Mooma. Their stories hold great significance and it is a clever technique employed by Pinnock, to take us back in time as well as nod to the future.

The Past
Colonialism beginning (early seventeenth century)
Slavery (1619–1837)
Nanny of the Maroons (early nineteenth century)
Windrush arrivals in the UK (1947–1972) Mai could have been in the first Windrush group
Enid's childhood in Jamaica and her relationship with her mother (1950s/'60s)
Brod's memories of Jamaica (1950/'60s)
Mai's marriage (early 1950s?)
Enid's marriage (late 1960s?)
Mai's relationship with her son (late 1960s/'70s?)
Enid's relationship with her husband in the UK (1970s?)
Gullyman's experiences in the UK (1970s?)

Viv and Del's early childhoods with Enid
Enid's experiences working for the NHS (mid 1970s/early '80s?)
Enid's last visit to Jamaica (1982)

The Future
Enid returning home for Mooma's funeral (1987)
Viv going to university (1987)
Del having her baby (1988)
The Windrush scandal

> *Context:* Turn to page 29 to read more about this 2018 political scandal.

A turning point

Pinnock structures the play around a key turning point in the **climax** at the end of Scene Three, when Enid learns about her mother's death.

At the start of the play, Enid has convinced herself that her sacrifices have been worth it, and whilst she has ties in Jamaica, her life and the future of her girls is in the UK. In the first few scenes, the 'truth' is presented through Brod and Del, but this is robustly challenged by Enid:

66 ENID. You come here, you try to fit in. Stick to the rules. England been good to me. I proud a my English girls. (Scene Two, page 29)

She is convinced that it is hard work, conformity and perseverance that will create access to being British.

Pinnock implies, however, that Enid is simply suppressing her true feelings. She is not keen for her children to delve into her past or connect with their culture.

The death of Mooma brings a serious change in perspective for Enid. Scene Four ends with Enid stating:

66 ENID. I want... I want to go home. (page 45)

'Home' is now Jamaica, and she tries to unpick her relationship with Mooma. We are almost fast-tracked through Enid's life and time in the UK as she reflects on the shattering of her optimism by a very grim reality. Pretending that things were better has created a lot of sadness and isolation, from British society, from her daughters, and from her connections and family in Jamaica. She is hopeful for Viv and concerned that Del will struggle. The passage of time sees Enid emerging as a woman who still has hopes and desires for herself. At the centre of this desire is feeling comfortable with missing 'home' and comfortable with admitting that the UK has been really difficult at times.

One further structural feature Pinnock uses is **dramatic irony**. An example of this appears in Scene Six when Enid worries to Mai about Del's whereabouts. The audience knows where Del is, as does Mai, and so the emotion of the scene and our sympathy is heightened.

Language: Voice and dialect

The way Pinnock uses language and **dialect** is an important aspect of the play. It is often said that older and younger people speak different languages, but this is heightened in the case of the Windrush generation and their UK-born children, as Pinnock shows.

Jamaican patois

The languages of the Caribbean have evolved out of key events in history. European colonisation of the Caribbean and the Americas led to the near extinctions of Indigenous languages and populations. The introduction of slavery saw the forced transportation of millions of West Africans who spoke a myriad of Niger-Conga languages, mostly lost over the course of slavery, through deliberate design (separating those who spoke the same language) and by insisting everyone spoke the dominant language which, depending on the colonisers, included:

- English
- Spanish
- French
- Dutch

What emerged were new languages and derivatives. These languages incorporated a grammatical system based on the Niger-Conga language group, mixed with the coloniser's tongue, and a smattering of words preserved from their own languages and that of the indigenous groups. The technical term for a new language born out of a combination of others is a '**creole**', while the term 'creolisation' also refers to the mixing of other cultural aspects, such as foods. The informal term most often used for the language of Jamaica is 'patois'.

Jamaican patois: a creole '**nation language**' draws on English as its basis, compared to the patois of Saint Lucia where French is the basis. There are degrees of density with patois, depending on whom one is talking to and the formality of the situation.

> Research the meaning of 'nation language' online.

In a school setting, Standard English (or Standard Jamaican English) would be the main form of communication. Talk amongst peers would be much more informal, and decidedly difficult for non-speakers to understand because of the shortening of words and the grammatical structure of sentences, as well as the use of words that aren't English. The infusion of youth culture and the emergence of phenomena such as **reggae**, **Rastafarianism**, and the movement of Caribbeans between islands and to the US and UK, for instance, has meant that patois continues to evolve and move with its originators as they in turn move across the globe.

> You can research reggae music and Rastafarianism online.

What Pinnock tries to do in the play is to capture this through the dialogue, without excluding a wider audience. She retains the flavour of patois but opts not to make it impenetrable, both in how it sounds and is written. This maintains authenticity whilst remaining accessible for the audience. What we hear more in the play is the '**accent**' of Jamaica, with flavours of the language and its grammatical turns. For example, the term 'unno', which means 'you', 'you all', 'any of you', is used by Mai in Scene One, on page 14. This is an important word used across the Caribbean, maintaining its original meaning and link to the West African Yoruba language.

We are not to assume that this is the only way these characters speak, and the time factor is also relevant, as Mai, Enid and Brod have been in the UK for decades. Like many Caribbean adult émigrés, they have not lost their accents, but for ease of communication, their language modifies, moving along the continuum. What the patois brings to the play and the experiences of the characters is the richness of their heritage.

How does the language you use to communicate with your friends differ from the way you write or speak in a formal situation? Do you speak another language or use terms from another language?

The London dialect

In contrast, Del and Viv speak a 'different' language, i.e. London English. Pinnock presents sisters raised together but with different grasps on the language and how they choose to use it. Through Del, we hear more informal language, such as 'the bass is mad', which is a merging of both cockney and the Caribbean London influence. This new form of **dialect** started amongst young Black British people but was and is used amongst their non-Black peers. Del feels disconnected from formal English because of her struggles with dyslexia and racism.

Viv's experience differs. She enjoys literature and the English language even though she begins to question its relevance to her life. She becomes more curious about her Caribbean culture. The sisters are able to find a common ground for communication which is informal, local and intimate. Just as with any other language, patois would be spoken in the home and be absorbed by children, many being able to speak it themselves. Del uses 'gyal' rather than 'girl' in Scene Five, and prefaces the Jamaican term 'duppies' with the English equivalent, 'evil spirits', in Scene One. In all, Pinnock demonstrates how cultures merge and diverge through the use and combining of different languages.

Essay Questions and How to Answer Them

In the exam, you will be expected to answer a question on:

- the whole text

and/or

- an extract from *Leave Taking*.

Exactly what you have to do depends on which exam board you are studying the text for. Details appear from page 11, but it's also always a good idea to pay close attention to the information your teacher shares with you about the exam so that you know what to expect.

You will be doing a lot of work around understanding exam questions and how best to tackle them. It's important not to panic – you have studied the play, enjoyed it, and gained an even greater understanding through the use of this guide.

A key strategy to use when you look at a question is *decoding*. Decoding is all about figuring out what you are being asked to do, by highlighting key words to ensure that your answer is precise.

Top Tip
AO1
You are being asked to refer closely to the text – this means that you need to look for specific examples.
AO2
Think about dramatic and literary devices. These are Pinnock's methods and techniques for conveying meaning – the tools she uses as a writer.

Let's look at a question:

How does Winsome Pinnock present characters' attitudes to the experience of living in the UK in *Leave Taking*?

Write about:

- The experiences of the characters in *Leave Taking*.

- How Pinnock presents their attitudes to these experiences by the way she writes.

So, what are you really being asked to do?

- You are being asked to focus on a key theme – the experience of life in the UK – and how the 'attitudes' of the characters help us to understand it.

- 'How' and 'present' are also keywords, which should get you thinking about the different ways in which Pinnock addresses this theme and the techniques employed.

Let's plan...

You need to work fast in an exam, however planning your answer is vital. Your plan will be your guide, and enable you to ensure that you address all the points that you intend to as you write and complete your response.

You will do plenty of timed essays in preparation, so as you go forward, get into the habit of numbering the points you make in your plan, and ticking them off as you address each one. You can also pace yourself by dividing up the time you will need to address each point. You will receive guidance on this in class. A plan will help you to complete the task in time, and you will get better at it with practice!

Step one: List your initial ideas

Make a brief list of key ideas that come to you following your decoding of the question, e.g.:

- Enid believing that life in Britain would offer greater opportunities for her and her children.

- Enid's change in attitude after Mooma's death.

- Broderick's scepticism of the UK and determination to keep ties with Jamaica.
- Viv feeling alienated from her own identity.
- Del's anger at discrimination she has experienced.
- Gullyman's desire to assimilate, and experience of racist abuse.

Step two: Add example moments/quotations from the play for each point

e.g.:

- Enid believing that life in Britain would offer greater opportunities for her and her children.

  'My daughter going to university. How many a my sister children back home going to university?' – Scene Two

Step three: Think about how you'll zoom in on your examples to analyse literary techniques

e.g.:

- Gullyman's desire to assimilate, and experience of racist abuse.

  'Gullyman heart brock, him mind crack, and now he can hardly talk broken English' – Scene Two

  Imagery: Pinnock uses **metaphor** and **onomatopoeia** ('heart brock', 'mind crack') to present Gullyman's mental pain as being sharply physical and audible. The ideas of being broken and cracked also suggest that this damage and the impact on Gullyman's feelings about living in the UK is permanent.

  > Keyword:
  > **Onomatopoeia** is a form of imagery when the sound of a word reflects its meaning.

Top Tip
When commenting on literary techniques, it is never enough just to name the technique – write about its impact and why Pinnock has chosen a particular device.

How to structure your response

Keyword: A **thesis statement** is a sentence that states what you believe in reference to the question, which you are going to use the evidence in your essay to prove.

Your essay needs to include an *introduction*, the points of analysis you have planned, arranged into *paragraphs*, and a *conclusion*. You should introduce your argument briefly at the start, by writing a **thesis statement**; then relate your points back to the claim you made in your thesis; and round off with a summary to conclude your argument at the end, ensuring that it offers your final answer to the question.

How to meet the Assessment Objectives

On page 10, you will find a table of Assessment Objectives which are used by the examiner to mark your work. Let's work through each one in turn and cover some tips for meeting them:

Assessment Objective 1

Read, understand and respond to texts. You should be able to:

- Maintain a critical style and develop an informed personal response.
- Use textual references, including quotations, to support and illustrate interpretations.

In other words…

- Make your points your own and don't be afraid to express ideas and thoughts you have explored and discussed in class.
- Use Standard English – avoid being chatty or informal.
- Always support your points by using examples, with references to parts of the text and, of course, quotations.

'Maintaining a critical style'

AVOID!
Viv says to Del that 'those teachers don't speak the same lingo' which tells us that Viv doesn't like her teachers.
Try this instead...
Pinnock presents Viv as being in conflict with her teachers, and feeling conflicted about her own academic success. When she says, 'Me and those teachers don't speak the same lingo', the use of the slang term 'lingo' emphasises how Viv understands the formal language of school but has another language too. Pinnock conveys Viv's need to be understood and to have her own culture recognised.

Experiment with the following words to express Pinnock's intentions and to show the effect her choices have:

Playwright	Critical Language Bank
Pinnock	suggests presents conveys explores implies examines shows how demonstrates illustrates describes outlines

Use 'we' when you are referring to the audience or readers of the play; what 'we' can do:

You! The critic/reader/audience	Critical Language Bank
We	infer recognise deduce understand perceive question see are given the impression reflect

Let's look at paragraphs from two students and note the differences:

Student A

Pinnock says[1] that Broderick has beef[2] with the UK government when he says that he will hold on to his Jamaican passport.[3] He says that he feels like he has been lied to and that his loyalty to Britain has been a waste of time. It also means that he feels disrespected.

1. Be precise: Pinnock doesn't actually *say* this, but she implies it in what Broderick says.

2. Informal language.

3. This is narrative rather than interpretation. Instead of analysing a quotation from the text, using literary terms to show how meaning is being conveyed, the student is simply describing what Broderick says.

Student B

Pinnock presents Broderick in Scene Two as deeply troubled by his experiences in the UK.[1] These feelings are illustrated when he recounts his experience as an immigrant, and ends by vowing to 'make sure me Jamaican passport up to date.'[2] This conveys his disappointment and distrust, with the passport becoming symbolic[3] of both belonging and feeling alienated. Pinnock implies that whilst on the surface Broderick seems very cheerful, his deeper thoughts and experiences have been more negative.[4]

1. A clear point describing how the writer presents the character.

2. A quotation to support the point, with critical language to show how it is relevant ('illustrated').

3. Literary analysis of symbolism.

4. Further analysis of the character, with varied critical vocabulary ('implies').

Student B will gain higher marks for their response, because they have attempted to look at the language choices Pinnock has made, quoted an appropriate example, and offered interpretation rather than narrative.

'Using textual references'

It is easy to fall into retelling the story, but this will only gain you minimal marks and use up time where you could be making very precise points and observations. At the heart of exam success is the effective and precise use of quotations.

1. Quote what is most useful.

2. Use quotation marks.

3. Quote accurately.

4. Longer quotations need to be set out correctly.

5. Shorter quotations should be embedded into your sentence in a way that is grammatically correct.

6. Avoid echoing your quote in what you go on to write – that's just saying it twice!

Using quotations is how you show your ability to focus on particular detail and language choices.

Student A
Pinnock presents Viv as a bright student,[1] showing this when Enid says proudly 'All 'A's, my daughter's going to university.'[2] The mention of the word 'university' suggests that Viv is set to do well in life[3] even though Pinnock describes Viv's needs beyond just being an 'A student'.[4]
1. Point is clear.
2. Quotation used is apt.
3. Explains the effect of the quotation.
4. This last idea is not sufficiently explained, but expanding on this could form the next point.

To reach the higher levels, your response needs to make a precise point linked to the relevant quotation, and then focus on specific words and phrases, explaining their effect or what is implied in order to make a broader point or draw inferences.

Student B

In the stage directions, Pinnock presents Viv as a conscientious student, demonstrating her dedication[1] as we see her with 'books balanced on her lap, making notes'.[2] The fact that Viv is not just reading but making notes reveals to us that she is studious, while the word 'balanced' implies that Viv studies wherever she can.[3] There is a suggestion through this, and Enid's later assertion of Viv achieving 'all 'A's', that this is intrinsic to Viv being highly regarded, and is why the savings account is set aside for Viv's future rather than Del's. The diligence in this scene-setting is countered by Viv's disillusioned feelings later in the play.[4]

1. Opens with a precise point.

2. Apt quotation, embedded in the sentence.

3. Explains the effect of language used, referring to specific words.

4. Draws inference, making a wider point about the character as well as the broader context of the play.

Assessment Objective 2

Let's try and break down Assessment Objective 2 so that we can understand it better.

We'll start by underlining some of the key things that are being assessed:

Analyse the language, form and structure used by the writer to create meanings and effects, using relevant subject terminology where appropriate.

In other words...

Question word	Decoding
analyse	You must write in detail about specific parts of the text and zoom in on quotations, commenting on choices made by the writer.
language	You should identify and comment on the effect of things like vocabulary, sentence structure, **imagery**, **dialect** and **tone**.

form	*Leave Taking* is a play, so how does its form affect the experience of the audience? Think about features that are specific to this form of text: dialogue, **stage directions**, settings.
structure	Think about the order of events, the introduction of characters and their final appearances, how the story unfolds and the characters and plot develop. Are there climaxes? As it is a play, it's divided into scenes – how does time pass through the play?
create meaning	Pinnock is trying to convey a number of themes to us through her writing of the play. What can we infer from the choices she has made in language, structure and form?
subject terminology	Technical terms – some of these relate to the form (drama), such as: **stage directions** or **monologue**, while others relate to literary techniques you might find in any set text, such as: **metaphor, simile, symbolism, foreshadowing, dramatic irony**, and so on. All the literary terms mentioned in this book appear in the glossary on page 171.

AVOID!

Del is very rude to Enid when she meets Mai so we know she doesn't like her much.

Try this instead...

Pinnock conveys Del's anger with her mother through the use of sarcasm and mimicry when she says, '"You two sit still and behave." She thinks we're seven years old.' Her tone of sarcasm suggests that Del objects to the way Enid treats her, but she refrains from displaying overt anger – opting instead for mimicking her words and voice. Tension is created as Enid is perhaps still in earshot, even though Del's remark is directed to Viv.

Three 'I' words to guide your responses

implied/implies/implication	infer/inferences/inferring	interpretation/interpret
Implying is what the author or characters do. Write about what is implied by what the playwright has written or what the characters say; by the choices of language, themes, ideas; and the events that are included or even left out!	Inferring is what we as critics, readers or audience do. We can see that Del is angry with Enid in Scene One, but what underlying meanings and clues can we infer? What does Del's anger suggest about the state of their relationship?	As you infer meaning, you will be able to form your own wider interpretation of the play, with specific ideas about its characters, themes and so on.

Assessment Objective 3

Assessment Objective 3 requires you to 'Show understanding of the relationships between texts and the contexts in which they were written.'

The Context chapter beginning on page 13 will help you with this.

When writing about context it is important to link your contextual ideas closely to your points and evidence, so they don't seem like an afterthought.

AVOID!

In Scene Two, Enid is angry with Del for staying out all night. Del says 'I like dancing. I been following that sound system for years.' Sound systems were popular among young people in the 1980s.

Try this instead...

Like many children of the Windrush generation in the 1980s, Del seeks to escape her frustration at injustice, and find a place to belong, by spending time with other young people like her and enjoying their shared culture. She upsets Enid by staying out all night dancing to music from the sound systems which were popular at the time, saying in Scene Two: 'When that bass gets inside you and flings you round the room you can't do nothing to stop it.'

Whether or not you need to address context in your answer depends on which exam board you are studying for. Check with your teacher whether you should be including points for AO3.

Assessment Objective 4

As well as using 'a range of vocabulary and sentence structures', Assessment Objective 4 is looking for correct spelling, punctuation and grammar, or 'SPAG'.

Spelling

Remember the correct spellings of:

- The author's name!
- Names of places.
- Names of characters.

Keep a list of words that you find tricky and refer to it often to check your spelling. It might be useful to arrange it in a chart and keep it in alphabetical order so that words are easy to find...

A	B	C
alliteration	Broderick	characterisation community
D	E	F

You can also write a list as part of your planning in the exam and check words off as you write, or at the end when you read over your work.

Punctuation and grammar

Precise sentences with correct punctuation help to keep your points clear.

Remember:

- Use full stops and commas in order to construct sentences with accuracy.

- Avoid sentences that are too long and may become nonsensical.
- Avoid very short sentences, as they are unlikely to be appropriate for the task in hand.
- Write fluently with the use of connecting words and phrases.
- Use inverted commas for quotations.

AVOID!
Scene Four opens and there is a shift of mood, the stage lighting changes from bright to dark, Enid is sat having a drink giving the impression that she is alone and grieving.
(Good points are made but the sentence is very long and list-like.)

Try this instead...
Scene Four opens signalling a shift of mood as the stage lighting changes to darkness. We are invited to look in on Enid and share her sense of grief and loss, as she reflects on the passing of Mooma.
(The same point is made through balanced sentences, correct punctuation and a focus on what is being presented to us.)

AVOID!
Although Del seemed to be an angry defiant teenager, Del's view of the world seemed to change for the better as Del built her new life at Mai's.
(Point made, but you should write in the present tense and use pronouns where appropriate. This will make your points less laboured!)

Try this instead...
Although Del seems to be an angry and defiant teenager, her view of the world seems to change for the better as she builds a new life at Mai's.
(Can you see the difference?)

More tips on SPAG

Although there are only a small number of marks set aside for spelling, punctuation and grammar, this could easily make the difference between one grade and another.

- Practise the spelling of key literary terms:

  irony   *character*   *theme*   *imagery*   *metaphor*
  protagonist   *climax*   *euphemism*   *simile*

  Put them in your chart!

- Vary the way you start your sentences. This will help to create a more interesting response. For example, instead of:

  'Enid is reluctant to send money to her sister in Jamaica but does so anyway.'

  try:

  'Despite her suspicions, Enid reluctantly continues to send money to her sister in Jamaica.'

OCR part a) – Comparing texts

If you are following the syllabus set by exam board OCR, then you will be required to compare an extract from *Leave Taking* with an unseen extract from another text that you have not studied. You will be familiar with the skill of comparison from your analysis of poems, and will find that this is a useful and transferrable skill.

When comparing, remember always to draw out the effect on the audience. What choices have the writers made, and what are their impacts?

Approaches to comparing texts

Model 1	Model 2	Model 3	Model 4
Close reading of text A. Close reading of text B. Comparison of A to B.	Comparison of themes. Comparison of styles. Analysis of differences.	Similarities found by exploring the form and context. Differences found by exploring language choices. Conclusion – evaluating and giving your opinion.	Close reading of text A. Compare A to B. Evaluative conclusion.

All of these models are acceptable approaches, and you may veer towards a particular one based on the question posed, or your preference.

All will require:

- A brief introduction and overview, addressing the question.

- A clear argument.

- Detailed analysis of both extracts, with balance between evaluation and close reading.

- A personal evaluation of both texts in your conclusion.

Turn to page 166 to see a sample question and answer for this essay, with some guidance on how to approach it.

Sample essays

This section will focus on three annotated sample answers to one exam question. This will enable you to see what is required across a range of levels.

Copy and complete the table below by reading each essay and then plotting the examiner's comments in a grid.

Can you see how each sample improves on the one before?

Which student are you closest to?

Note down some targets for improvement, using the comments and pointers you have learned from reading the essays.

Student A	Student B	Student C
Introduces the basic characteristics.	Introduction is clear and outlines key points.	Focused opening presenting characters importance to text.
Target for improvement...		

Question:

How does Pinnock use the character of Mai to explore ideas about friendship?

Write about:

- What Mai says and does.

- How Pinnock uses Mai to explore ideas about friendship.

Student A

Pinnock presents Mai as a woman who seems reluctant to even do her job because it is a Bank Holiday. So when we first meet her, she seems to be unfriendly but as the play goes on Mai's role as a friend is shown to us.

Mai is an obeah woman which means she cares for the wellbeing of people. She seems to be quite alone but she is important in her community and lots of women visit her for advice. She gets annoyed and says 'they think I can work miracles' because people visit for help with the 'Mirror Bingo' and relationship problems. We also find out that she doesn't see her son and that there was conflict between them.

Mai is visited by everyone in the play looking for advice and the benefit of her powers, like they did in Jamaica as obeah was an important practice there. But she actually starts to become a friend to both Enid and Del.

At first it seems that all Mai cares about is being paid but we see the beginning of her friendliness to Enid as she gives advice about Del, 'you should go to bed' advising that Del needs to find her own way. Later in the play, Mai is really loving towards Enid and as Enid tries to pay Mai says, 'Nuttin. I give as a friend' showing us her compassion. She also uses dialect here to maybe show how she feels and to connect with Enid.

Mai also establishes a friendship with Del and even though Del doesn't like Mai much in the beginning, she realises she can turn to Mai on leaving home. Mai also becomes a mother figure to Del.

Overall Pinnock uses Mai to explore friendship because it was so important for immigrants who had left everyone at home and it was a way to maintain their culture.

Student A

Commentary

- This student shows understanding of Mai and makes basic points referencing how friendship is explored.

- Paragraphs are effectively structured.

- Vocabulary is limited and some expressions are too informal.

- There are only basic references to context.

To move up

- This student needs to adopt a more formal style with a broader range of vocabulary, and avoid slang.

- Writing about the effects Pinnock creates needs to be done explicitly with references to literary devices – show how Pinnock creates effect from language choices.

- They should embed quotations so that they flow within a sentence.

- They should avoid retelling the story in great detail.

- They should make greater reference to context.

Whether or not you need to address context in your answer depends on what exam board you are studying for. Check with your teacher whether you should be including points for AO3.

Student B

Mai is presented to us as an obeah woman, a role that is central in the Caribbean community and a strong link to traditions back home in Jamaica. Pinnock presents Mai in a number of roles throughout the play, and the seeds of her role as a 'friend' begin in Scene One.

At the start of the play Mai is reluctant to welcome Enid and the girls, but quickly moves into business mode, charging 'ten pounds extra on top a the special Bank Holiday price', and the effect is to make us view Mai as an opportunist. She builds an atmosphere of mysticism and talent around herself and talks about being able to 'see right through to your soul' which is a strong image that Pinnock creates to persuade Enid, the girls and the audience of her powers.

We learn that Mai is alone and whilst she is keen to be businesslike, her true character comes to the surface as she attempts to offer advice and help to both Enid and Del. She could easily create a divide between Enid and Del, but Pinnock shows us how Mai steps in as a friend and offers shelter to Del but encourages her to return home. Her role as a mother figure and friend of the family is important in the Caribbean community as many family members were left behind in Jamaica.

Mai not only trains Del to take over from her but also teaches Del life lessons about how to behave when she says, 'You want to stay here in my house you abide by my rules' using 'rules' and 'abide' as a way of teaching the importance of respect and what would be expected of Del in her community. Mai also helps Del to acknowledge her problems with reading, describing how the words 'run across the page like black ants', showing through this simile how and why Del struggles. Mai is able to act as a friend on many levels towards Del, and Pinnock shows us how this is important for Del's growth and gives Mai a chance to improve on her outcome with her own son.

With Enid, Mai is also able to do better as a parent through her advice. The contrast with her added prices at the start of the play is marked when we see Mai turn into a friend offering advice and support for free. Through her second reading with Enid, a bond is established, and Pinnock conveys to us how their pain regarding life in the UK and raising children is a shared experience. The stage directions present Enid in a 'howl of pain' almost as if to echo a very base and animalistic response in order to show her despair and anguish. Mai supports and consoles her when Enid asks how much to pay her – Mai says 'Nuttin. I give as a friend,' showing the audience that their bond has deepened.

Pinnock explores the role of friendship by highlighting how Mai is able to offer support and a cultural link to 'back home'. She also shows cross-generational friendships as Mai is much older than Enid and Del. Pinnock also shows how friendship links to a central theme of family and its various presentations in the play.

Commentary

- This is a confident response.

- The student shows a good understanding of character, motivations and ideas of friendship.

- There is identification of literary devices.

- There is some exploration of language to emphasise effects.

- Relevant quotations have been embedded into sentences.

- There is reference to context.

- Sometimes, language is informal.

To move up

- This student needs to include greater detail and precise comment on Mai's behaviour and motives.

- Deeper analysis of literary techniques is needed.

- Points linking to other aspects of the play, such as conflict between generations and cultural identity, could be expanded on but should also be linked very clearly to the main focus of the question: the answer should tackle 'friendship' more directly and explicitly.

- The student should experiment with a broader range of sophisticated vocabulary and sentence structure to describe character and to drive the premise of the essay.

Student C

The centrality of obeah within Caribbean communities transported to the UK helped to provide a bridge between 'home' and life in a foreign country. Whilst there is great emphasis on Mai's role as an obeah woman, Pinnock encourages us to look beyond obeah when it comes to Mai's relationship with Enid and Del. Through Mai, Pinnock explores how the establishing of new friendships offers vital support in transposed communities, and how friendship connects to themes of family and cultural identity.

Pinnock uses the character of Mai to explore the multiple layers of friendship, and how the Windrush generation leant into the bonds made with others in their situation. The audience's initial introduction to Mai is dictated by the stage directions, creating an image of an old woman in 'very messy' surroundings. However, Pinnock intentionally presents Mai to the audience in a chaotic manner that is opposite to the role she goes on to play. As the play progresses, Pinnock depicts Mai as wise and steady in the role of adviser, using her life experiences to steer Enid onto a better path with Del. This is over and above her practice as an obeah woman, and when Mai talks of being able to 'read into your soul', Pinnock's metaphor creates an image that is layered, as culturally, Mai is able to relate to Enid and Del through shared experiences as well as through her gift.

In Scene Six we see Mai bonding and empathising with Enid, and sharing snapshots of her own life, which allows Enid to open up. Pinnock's stage directions then describe Enid's 'howl', signalling a sense of primal pain and inviting the audience to see and hear Enid's despair, anguish and desperation. Pinnock employs dramatic irony as we, the audience, know that Del is staying with Mai when Enid says 'I don't know where she is', but we see in the tenderness and sadness of the scene (and Mai later imploring Del to go after Enid), that Mai's intentions are genuine. Through Mai, Pinnock explores the challenge of offering friendship and support simultaneously to two people in conflict.

Mai can arguably be seen as a mother figure to both Enid and Del, and it is as if Pinnock is attempting to convey to us that friendship is lacking in other examples of mother/child relationships. Mai atones for her lack of understanding of her son's plight by listening to Del and trying to establish 'rules' around their friendship that Del needs to 'abide' by. The noun 'rules' and verb 'abide' with their semantic field of regulation emphasise the discipline required for maintaining friendships and respecting others.

Honesty also becomes an intrinsic aspect of friendship, and Mai's ability to home in on Del's dyslexia is a key moment in our understanding of Del. Pinnock uses a simile 'like black ants' to illustrate Mai's empathy, and evoke for the audience a sense of words literally escaping Del at speed. The development of their friendship transcends the generational divide and Pinnock crafts the dialogue between them, authentically displaying Del's London dialect with the use of 'mumbo-jumbo' as a euphemism and metaphor for obeah, with Mai's steady and deliberate use of patois. The repetition of 'wrong' in the phrase 'if me wrong say me wrong' followed by Del echoing it, shows how they begin to feed off each other as they communicate and strengthen their bond.

In conclusion, Pinnock skilfully constructs Mai's character to serve as a symbol of friendship, family ties and how a shared experience can create friendships and the support mechanisms needed to uphold notions of identity and belonging.

Student C

Commentary

- This a high-level critique of Mai's behaviour and motives.

- There is effective and comfortable use of literary techniques, and analysis of language and its impact on the audience, as well as Pinnock's intentions.

- Links are made to other aspects of the play, such as conflict between generations and cultural identity.

- There is a range of sophisticated vocabulary to describe character and to drive the premise of the essay.

- There is a good variety of sentence structures.

- The conclusion is highly effective as it addresses Mai's importance and the centrality of cultural practices in the play.

More practice essay questions

How does Pinnock use Brod to explore ideas about masculine identity in *Leave Taking*?

Write about:

- What Brod says and does.

- How Pinnock uses Brod to explore ideas about masculine identity.

How far does Pinnock present Enid as a strong female character in *Leave Taking*?

Write about:

- What Enid says and does.

- How far Pinnock presents Enid as a strong female character.

How does Pinnock use Del to explore ideas about racism in *Leave Taking*?

Write about:

- What Del says and does.
- How Pinnock uses Del to explore ideas about racism.

Write about belonging and how Pinnock presents this at various points in the play.

In your response you should:

- Choose and refer to an extract, and the play as a whole.
- Show your understanding of characters and events in the play.

Write about family and how Pinnock presents this at various points in the play.

In your response you should:

- Choose and refer to an extract, and the play as a whole.
- Show your understanding of characters and events in the play.

Explore a moment in *Leave Taking* where there is guilt or betrayal.

You should refer to a specific extract and the play as a whole.

Explore a moment in *Leave Taking* where a character is learning and changing.

You should refer to a specific extract and the play as a whole.

OCR comparison sample essay

Leave Taking could be compared with a play called *Princess & The Hustler* by Chinonyerem Odimba, so this sample will compare these two texts. However, the guidance offered will be useful to you whatever extract you are given in the exam.

Read the two extracts below and then answer the question.

Extract 1 from: *Leave Taking* by Winsome Pinnock

In this extract, Enid has been preparing for the arrival of the Pastor and his wife, and Viv has been studying on the sofa. Brod has arrived, wearing a suit and tie, and has been reminiscing about 'back home' in Jamaica, and what has happened since he came to the UK. He tells Viv about his friend Gullyman.

BROD (*to Viv*). Gullyman come over here with two dollar in him pocket. But Gullyman could work, and he had a talent for saving. Within three years Gullyman buy car – old car granted, but car all the same – an' house. Gullyman forget everybody – all him friends, him people back home, just cut everybody off. You meet him in the road, him wouldn't see you. Too high. Remember how him use to talk, Enid?

ENID. Like him have cork in him nose hole.

BROD. An' he was always correcting people. 'Don't say wartar, man. Say wortur.' One mornin Gullyman wake up to find him lovely car covered in shit an a message on him door read 'wogs out'. Gullyman heart brock, him mind crack, and now he can hardly talk broken English.

VIV. That's sad, man.

BROD. English.

ENID. You come here, you try to fit in. Stick to the rules. England been good to me. I proud a my English girls.

BROD. You teaching these children all wrong. They going forget where them come from. These girls ain't English like them newsreader who got English stamp on them like the letters on a stick a rock, right through English. These girls got Caribbean souls.

VIV. Don't you mean African souls?

ENID. Don't talk foolish. African...

BROD. Girl, you a 'A'-class student... Tell me what you know about Nanny a the Maroons.

VIV. Never heard of her.

Extract 2 from: *Princess and the Hustler* by Chinonyerem Odimba

In this extract, teenaged Wendell Junior has just lashed out at his father Wendell, who has returned to the family after abandoning them many years ago.

WENDELL. Junior yuh gon' 'ave tark* to me man to man some time?
Mi* need to explain some tings to yuh /

WENDELL JUNIOR. You know what they call a boy without a father round here?
Do you?
Bastard!
A bloody bastard! /

WENDELL. Mi beg yuh stop!
When mi come to dis country I was ar good man.
Ar soldier.
Fight far King an' country.
But it never make far respec'.
Fram* dis Englishman.
Dem* just throw mi out of the army, and expect mi to live on air.
Mi try to make it work for all af us.
Truly.
But here...

Beat.

Even now everywhere mi go looking far work, dem look at mi so so...
An' grown men wit ar family scratching around far even ar paper round.

Wha' kinda world?!
Wha' kinda world put men in de same sentence as dogs?
Supm* 'ave ta change fram de days of mi ancestors.
'Ave ta!

WENDELL *pours himself a large drink –*

WENDELL JUNIOR. Why have you come back? It still the same.
Nothing is different /

WENDELL. Mi trying to tark to yuh straight…

WENDELL JUNIOR. Sounds like excuses to me.

WENDELL. Excuses?

WENDELL JUNIOR. Lots of excuses.

WENDELL JUNIOR *gets up to leave –*

WENDELL. Yuh nuh live yet.
Yuh young'un still.
One day yuh understand.

Glossary
* tark = talk
* mi = I/me
* fram = from
* dem = them
* supm = something

Compare how both extracts present characters experiencing disappointment.

You should consider:

* The situations and experiences faced by the characters.

* How the characters react to the situations and experiences.

* How language and dramatic features create effects.

You should focus only on the extracts here rather than referring to the rest of your studied text.

Example response

Odimba and Pinnock present characters who experience disappointment in compelling and moving ways. Through a device of storytelling, Pinnock has Brod relate Gullyman's experience, whilst also feeding Brod's own disappointment into the extract. Meanwhile, Odimba employs a mixture of dialogue and poetic monologue to convey the disappointments of son and father, across generations.

Odimba contrasts the language of Wendell Junior and Wendell as we see their exchange unfold in Wendell's patois and Wendell Junior's local English. It could be argued that this represents a barrier between them, but the mode of communication also serves to best share how much hurt both characters feel. Wendell Junior challenges his father with a question, 'You know what they call a boy without a father round here?' and his tone of anger and frustration is reinforced as he demands: 'Do you?' before answering the question himself. The question is rhetorical as Odimba does not include a 'pause' or 'beat' for Wendell to respond: Wendell Junior simply needs the opportunity to express his disappointment in his father.

Wendell's disappointment becomes a poetic monologue, expressing his feelings about the impact of racism and prejudice. Like Wendell Junior, he uses rhetorical questions to emphasise the hurt he feels as he says 'Wha' kinda world put men in de same sentence as dogs?' This question is a nod to the racial tensions of the time. Odimba is concerned with engaging the audience in Wendell's disappointment, which is tempered by Wendell Junior's anguish. Wendell tries to share how emasculated he feels by society, but Wendell Junior challenges and reminds Wendell of his responsibilities to his children, saying 'Sounds like excuses to me'. We feel sympathy for both characters as the tension is built effectively. For example, when the stage directions dictate that Wendell 'pours himself a large drink', we know by the adjective 'large' that Wendell is under pressure and stressed. Throughout the extract, we sense the difficulty both characters have in expressing what they have experienced, and whilst they may not understand each other, the audience is left in no doubt of their individual disappointment.

Pinnock takes up a similar stance in Extract 1 by homing in on the effects of racism. Just like Wendell's, Brod's tale points to Gullyman's determination to capitalise on opportunities in the UK. Pinnock's characterisation of Gullyman differs from Odimba's of Wendell, in that Gullyman was prepared to 'forget everybody – all him friends' in order to succeed and fit in to British society.

This contrasts with Wendell's determination to 'fight far King an' country' demonstrating a deep yearning to belong. In both extracts we see that their attempts and approaches end in disappointment.

Pinnock takes the impact of disappointment further than Odimba as Brod eerily points to Gullyman's mental breakdown, using the onomatopoeic words 'brock' and 'crack' to present his mental pain as being sharply physical and audible. It could be argued that the impact of disappointment clearly hits Wendell deeply too, as he abandons his family. Pinnock uses Gullyman's story as a warning, and we see Brod pleading with Enid not to allow the girls to forget their 'Caribbean souls'. This term is possibly employed to emphasise the importance of identity when all else is lost. The audience can see Brod's pleasure in Viv's interest when he says 'Girl, you a 'A'-class student', but we can infer his disappointment on learning that Viv has 'never heard' of 'Nanny a the Maroons'. Like Odimba, Pinnock explores a disconnection between the two generations; however, unlike Wendell Junior who 'gets up to leave', Viv appears to show interest in Brod's topic of cultural identity.

In these extracts, both Pinnock and Odimba convey to their audience the importance of having a sense of identity and pride as a crucial form of protection against a backdrop of racism. The hope in Pinnock's portrayal of disappointment is represented by Viv, while Odimba depicts Wendell trying to make amends for allowing his disappointment to cloud his responsibilities to his family.

Commentary

- A high-level answer.
- Well structured, seamlessly contrasting and comparing the way the writers deal with similar themes.
- Detailed analysis and examples of the writers' methods.
- Precise references woven into the main body of the essay.
- Some reference to context across both plays.
- Impact on audience effectively addressed.
- Offers interpretations.
- Spelling and punctuation is accurate with a considerable range of vocabulary.
- Sentence structures are clear and varied.

Glossary

An **accent** is the way words are pronounced, and differs according to location.

An **adjective** is a describing word for a noun.

An **allegory** is a story with a hidden (typically moral or political) meaning.

Anglophone means English speaking.

Assimilate means to behave in a 'similar' way in order to fit in.

A **catalyst** is a person or thing that causes an event.

Colloquialisms are informal terms used within particular communities.

Colourism refers to the idea that lighter skin is more desirable because of its closer proximity to European ideals of beauty.

The **Commonwealth** was formed in 1949 to maintain the relationship between The British Empire and its former colonies. Its membership is voluntary, with fifty-six members in 2023. King Charles III is the head of the Commonwealth succeeding Queen Elizabeth II, and remains the official head of state of many of these countries.

Contrast is used for effect by writers, to emphasise the differences between people, places or things. It is also an effective technique to draw contrasts in your own essays.

Creole is a language formed from the blending of two or more languages.

Dialect is the words used which are specific to a location, such as London, or Jamaica.

Diaspora is the dispersion or spread of a people from their original homeland.

Dramatic irony is when information known to the reader or audience is not known to the character(s) in a scene.

Exaggeration and **hyperbole** are English and Greek words meaning almost the same thing – but 'hyperbole' is particularly used when writing about literary technique: it means 'exaggeration used for effect'.

Expletives are swear words.

Exposition is where key information about characters and context is established.

Foreshadowing is when a moment in the story hints at something that will happen later.

Hyperbole is exaggeration for effect.

Imagery is when writers use language to paint pictures in the audience's mind. **Metaphors** and **similes** are examples of imagery, as is **personification**.

Irony is when something said or a moment in the plot is deliberately the opposite of what is expected.

A **metaphor** is a form of imagery where a thing is described indirectly by referring to something it resembles, without using 'like'.

Mirroring is when writers repeat images of moments, or behaviour, from character to character.

A **monologue** is a long speech spoken by a single character.

Mother Country is the country that possesses or possessed a colony or former colony. For example, under the old British Empire, England was Jamaica's 'Mother Country'.

A **nuclear family** is the traditional family unit of a mother, father and their children.

Onomatopoeia is a form of imagery when the sound of a word reflects its meaning.

Oral tradition is when knowledge and culture is received and passed on in spoken (or sung) form, from generation to generation.

Ostracisation is the social shunning or shutting-out of a person.

Othering is the act of treating someone as though they are not part of a group and are in some way different.

A **paradox** is something that seems to have contradictory qualities.

Personification is when something non-human is written about as if it has human characteristics.

A **plot device** is a technique designed to move the narrative forward.

Props are objects used on stage by actors. The word is short for 'properties'.

Repetition is a literary technique often used by writers for emphasis.

Rhetorical questions are questions that do not expect an answer but are instead intended to make the listener think about what the answer would be. They are a very persuasive and impactful literary technique.

A **simile** is a form of imagery where something is described as resembling something else. It is usually signalled with the word 'like' or 'as'.

A **soliloquy** is when a character speaks their thoughts aloud, either alone onstage or without any other characters who are onstage hearing or responding.

Speaking in tongues is when people utter speech-like sounds or words of an unknown language during a heightened state as part of religious worship.

Stage directions are written into playtexts to tell the director and actors what should happen physically on stage.

Subtext means information that is suggested by the words on the page, without being said directly.

Symbolism is when symbols are used to represent ideas.

A **thesis statement** is a sentence that states what you believe in reference to the question, which you are going to use the evidence in your essay to prove.

Tone is the way in which a writer or speaker conveys their attitude to what they are saying.

Unbelonging is a feeling of not belonging in a place, group of people, or culture.

Womanist is a term coined by Alice Walker to describe 'a Black feminist or feminist of colour'.

Further Reading and Research

Books

Windrush by Trevor Phillips

Home coming: Voices of the Windrush Generation by Colin Grant

Mother Country by Charlie Brinkhurst-Cuff

Waiting in the Twilight by Joan Riley

Maybe I Don't Belong Here: A Memoir of Race, Identity, Breakdown and Recovery by David Harewood

Post Traumatic Slave Syndrome by Dr Joy DeGruy

Natives: Race and Class in the Ruins of Empire by Akala

Caste: The Origins of Our Discontents by Isabel Wilkerson

Other authors you may like to read

Louise Bennett

Buchi Emecheta

Lorna Goodison

Andrea Levy

Chinonyerem Odimba

Sam Selvon

Olive Senior

TV and Film

Red, White and Blue (2020)

Sitting in Limbo (2020)

Small Axe (2021)

Three Little Birds (2023)

Web links

Links to a variety of useful sites for further contextual reading, past reviews of the play, audio recordings, interviews, and exam-board information, can all be found on this book's dedicated webpage: www.nickhernbooks.co.uk/leave-taking-study-guide-further-resources